PACEMAKER'S ®

PASSAGE TO

Basic English

GLOBE FEARON

Pearson Learning Group

Director Editorial & Marketing, Special Education: Diane Galen
Market Manager: Susan McLaughlin
Executive Editor: Joan Carrafiello
Project Editor: Stephanie Petron Cahill
Contributing Editors: Amy Jolin, Jennifer McCarthy, Elena Petron
Editorial Development: Lake Publishing, Inc.
Editorial Assistants: Derrell Bradford, Ryan Jones
Production Director: Kurt Scherwatzky
Production Editor: John Roberts
Art Direction and Cover Design: Pat Smythe, Armondo Baez
Page Design: Margarita Giammanco
Electronic Page Production: Jose Lopez

Teacher Reviewers:

Beth Bina Carlson,
Special Needs Teacher,
Central High,
Grand Forks, North Dakota

Carolyn Lambert,
Special Education Teacher,
Lower Pioneer Valley Educational Collaborative,
Wilbraham, Massachusetts

Dorie L. Knaub, BS, MA.,
Consultant,
Downey Unified School District,
Downey, California

ISBN 0-8359-3463-2
Printed in the United States of America

10 11 12 13   07 06

1-800-321-3106
www.pearsonlearning.com

Contents

Note to the Student 1

Unit 1: Sentences and Punctuation

    Lesson **1** What Is a Sentence? 2

             2 Subjects and Predicates 4

             3 End Punctuation 6

             4 Commas 8

             5 Commas in a Series 10

             6 Commas That Set Off Words 12

             7 Direct Quotations 14

             8 Dates and Place Names 16

             9 Colons, Semicolons, and Hyphens 18

Unit 2: Nouns

    Lesson **10** What Is a Noun? 20

          11 Proper Nouns 22

          12 Regular Plural Nouns 24

          13 Irregular Plural Nouns 26

          14 Possessive Nouns 28

Unit 3: Pronouns

    Lesson **15** Personal Pronouns 30

          16 Reflexive Pronouns 32

          17 Possessive Pronouns 34

          18 Indefinite Pronouns 36

          19 Interrogative and Demonstrative Pronouns 38

Unit 4: Verbs

Lesson **20** What Is a Verb? 40

21 Linking Verbs. 42

22 Present Tense Verbs. 44

23 Regular Past Tense Verbs 46

24 Irregular Past Tense Verbs 48

25 *To Be* Verb Phrases 50

26 *To Have* Verb Phrases 52

27 *To Do* Verb Phrases 54

28 Using *Not* with Verbs. 56

29 Future Tense Verbs 58

30 Other Helping Verbs 60

31 Direct and Indirect Objects 62

Unit 5: Adjectives and Adverbs

Lesson **32** What Is an Adjective? 64

33 Adjectives After Linking Verbs 66

34 Proper Adjectives 68

35 Comparative Adjectives 70

36 Irregular Comparative Adjectives 72

37 What Is an Adverb? 74

38 Adjective Modifiers 76

39 Adverb Modifiers 78

40 When to Use an Adverb or an Adjective. 80

41 Avoiding Double Negatives 82

Unit 6: Sentences

Lesson **42** Conjunctions and Sentence Parts 84

43 Simple Sentences. 86

44 Compound Sentences. 88

Glossary 90

Note to the Student

Reading, writing, and speaking are important for living and working with others. These communication skills come from good use of English. *Passage to Basic English* teaches the meaning of a sentence and the parts of a sentence. You will also learn how to use different phrases and sentences. All of these important skills are taught in small parts that are easy to understand. When you finish, you will have the tools it takes to succeed in communicating with others.

Each lesson of *Passage to Basic English* starts with Words to Know. This section shows you words you may not have seen before. Then, when you see them in the lesson, you will have some idea of what they mean.

The lessons have small parts. They are named by letters. Each part teaches you something new through clear examples. Every part also contains exercises. Exercises ask you to use what you have just learned. As you do them, you can show your work and answers on a separate sheet of paper.

There are other study aids in the lessons, too. Reminders point out things you might need to be able to follow the examples. Other notes in the margin give you helpful hints.

We wish you well on your *Passage to Basic English.* Our success comes from your success.

Lesson 1

What Is a Sentence?

Words to Know

sentence a group of words that makes sense
capital letter a letter written in upper case
period (.) a dot at the end of a sentence

The word *sentence* sounds like SEN-tens.

A. A **sentence** tells a complete thought. This means that the sentence makes sense. Think about what a group of words is saying. Do you understand it? Does it make sense?

a sentence ⟶ The fish swam.

If it does not make sense, it is not a sentence. Look at the example below. What do you know about the fish? It does not make sense. It is not a sentence.

not a sentence ⟶ The fish.

Read each group of words. Rewrite only the sentences.
1. Gina's little sister takes piano lessons.
2. Takes piano lessons.
3. Luke plays baseball and football.
4. Baseball and football.
5. Amy ran up and down the street.
6. Up and down the street.
7. High in the sky.
8. The kite flew high in the sky.
9. A walk in the park.
10. I took a walk in the park.

B. A sentence always begins with a **capital letter**. A capital letter is written in upper case. A sentence can end with a **period**. A period is a dot at the end of some sentences. Look at the example below. The first word begins with a capital *T*. The end of the sentence has a period.

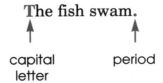

The fish swam.

↑ capital letter ↑ period

Write each sentence correctly. Be sure to begin with a capital letter and end with a period.

Reminder

Write your sentences on a separate piece of paper.

1. she ran fast
2. he felt bad
3. jerome likes books
4. i read the letter

C. Sometimes a group of words looks like a sentence. But, the words don't make sense. If so, it may only be part of a sentence. Look at the examples below.

> **sentence part** ⟶ if that cat howls all night

> **a sentence** ⟶ I will never get to sleep, if that cat howls all night.

Read each group of words. Use words from the box to make each sentence part into a sentence.

Reminder

A sentence tells a complete thought.

I laugh	he will pass.
She wore shorts	We have practice

1. when you tell a joke.
2. If he studies,
3. because it was hot.
4. every Monday.

D. There are four kinds of sentences. Each kind of sentence does a different job. A sentence:

- **tells about something** ⟶ Dan drove the car.
- **asks a question** ⟶ Did Dan drive the car?
- **gives a command** ⟶ Drive faster, Dan.
- **shows strong feeling** ⟶ Dan is a great driver!

Read each sentence. Write what each sentence does. Choose from the kinds of sentences described in the box.

• tells about something	• asks a question
• gives a command	• shows strong feeling

1. Did you call Susan tonight?
2. Stop the car.
3. This is a beautiful park!
4. That family lives on our street.

Lesson 2 Subjects and Predicates

Words to Know

subject the part of a sentence that tells who or what the sentence is about.

predicate the part of a sentence that tells what the subject *does* or *is*

All sentences have two main parts. If one of these parts is missing, the group of words is not a sentence.

A. Look at the sentence below. You can find the part that tells who or what the sentence is about. This is called the **subject** of the sentence. Some sentences *tell about something*. In these sentences, the subject is usually the first part.

Reminder

There are four kinds of sentences. They can *tell about something, ask a question, give a command,* or *show strong feeling.*

The twins dress alike.
↑
subject

Some sentences *give a command*. In these sentences, the subject may not be written or spoken. It is understood to be whoever you're talking to. The subject is always *you* or whoever you're speaking to.

(You) Run!
↑
subject

Read each sentence. Write what the subject is for each sentence.
1. The dogs ran into the park.
2. They stopped to dig up flowers.
3. Get out of there!

B. In other kinds of sentences, it may be harder to find the subject. How do you find the subject in these kinds of sentences?

asks a question ⟶ Did Matt read his mail?

shows strong feeling ⟶ What blue eyes the baby has!

It often helps to move the words around. You can turn a sentence that *asks a question* into a sentence that *tells about something*.

asks a question ⟶ Did Matt read his mail?

tells about something ⟶ Matt did read his mail.

You also can turn a sentence that *shows strong feeling* into a sentence that *tells about something*. Notice that you may have to leave out a word or two.

shows strong feeling ⟶ What blue eyes the baby has!

tells about something ⟶ The baby has blue eyes.

Move words around to make each into a sentence that *tells*. Rewrite the new sentence. Underline the subject in each sentence.

1. What a delicious dessert Jan made!
2. Has Al finished his math homework?
3. Will Tammy sell me her car?
4. Why haven't you left yet?

C. The **predicate** tells what the subject *does* or *is*. Finding a predicate is easy. All the words that are not the subject are part of the predicate. You know about sentences that *tell about something*. In these sentences, the predicate is usually the second part.

The Yankees <u>won the game</u>.
predicate

That farmer <u>grows corn, beans, and tomatoes</u>.

The word *predicate* sounds like PREH-dih-kuht.

Reminder

Every sentence has two main parts: a subject and a predicate.

Rewrite each sentence. Underline the subject. Circle the predicate for each.

1. The sun hurt our eyes.
2. My baseball cap is dirty already.
3. My family had a great vacation!
4. The broken lawn chair was fixed by Stan.
5. The yellow flowers are my favorite.
6. The dolphin jumped out of the water.
7. Jane and Jimmy walked to school.
8. The crowd cheered loudly.

Lesson 3   End Punctuation

Words to Know

punctuation marks in a sentence to make writing clearer

question mark (?) a mark that shows a sentence is a question

exclamation point (!) a mark that shows a sentence shows strong feeling

The word *punctuation* sounds like punk-choo-WAY-shuhn.

All **punctuation** marks make your writing clearer. They help you know when to slow down or stop reading. End punctuation shows where one sentence ends and another begins. Always notice end punctuation. It shows you when a thought has been completed.

Are you ready for the party? It starts at four o'clock. What a surprise it will be for Michael!

Reminder

Every sentence begins with a capital letter. A period is a dot at the end of a sentence.

A. Different kinds of sentences use different kinds of end punctuation. Most sentences end with a period. A sentence that asks a question ends with a **question mark (?)**. A sentence that shows strong feeling ends with an **exclamation point (!)**. Read the rules below.

- If a sentence tells what something *does* or *is,* it ends with a period.

  This is a hot day.

- If a sentence makes a mild command, it ends with a period.

  Please turn on the fan.

- If a sentence asks a question, it ends with a question mark.

  How hot is it?

- If a sentence shows strong feeling, it ends with an exclamation point.

  What a hot day this is!

- If a sentence gives a strong command, it ends with an exclamation point.

  Turn off that fan!

Read each sentence. Decide what kind of sentence it is. Does the end punctuation fit the meaning of the sentence? Rewrite only the sentences that have correct end punctuation.

1. Have you ever seen a canary?
2. A canary is a small, yellow songbird!
3. Canaries are sold in pet stores.
4. The pet store owner knows all about canaries.
5. She said that a canary has about 2000 feathers?

B. End punctuation helps a reader understand what you have written. A period shows that you are telling something or giving a mild command. A question mark shows that you are asking something. An exclamation point shows that you are giving a strong command or showing strong feeling.

Rewrite the sentences correctly. Begin each sentence with a capital letter. End each sentence with the correct punctuation mark. The first one has been done for you.

1. where is Patrick going to college
   Where is Patrick going to college?
2. how sad I was to hear your news
3. pass the salt, please
4. my brother works at the shoe store
5. i am learning to play chess
6. jump
7. do you know where the zoo is

Reminder

Write your sentences on a separate sheet of paper.

C. Imagine trying to read a story that had no end punctuation. It would not be easy. All the thoughts would run into each other.

no end punctuation ⟶ Have you ever been to Honolulu what a beautiful beach Waikiki is the beach is almost two miles long

correct end punctuation ⟶ Have you ever been to Honolulu? What a beautiful beach Waikiki is! The beach is almost two miles long.

Write two sentences from each group of words. Begin each sentence with a capital letter. Use the correct end punctuation.

1. did you see the mountain it is covered with snow
2. what a day I had I had to stand in lines for hours
3. my dog jumped into a stream she was covered in mud
4. the bus just left when can I get another
5. i am going to the store do you need milk
6. i drive a blue car it is parked outside

Lesson 4 Commas

pause to slow down for a moment without stopping

comma (,) a punctuation mark that tells when to pause between words or word groups

Reminder

A punctuation mark is used in a sentence to help make writing clearer.

Sometimes when you are reading you need to slow down but not stop. This is a **pause** in the sentence. Certain marks of punctuation tell the reader when to pause.

A **comma** is one kind of punctuation that tells you where to pause, or slow down. Commas also separate words or word groups within a sentence.

A. When you speak, you sometimes pause in the middle of a sentence. You do this to show a break in your thought. When you write, you can use a comma to show a pause. The comma divides a sentence into different word groups. This makes your writing clearer.

On the day before her birthday, Ramona got the flu.

Read each sentence. Notice where there is a break in thought. Rewrite the sentence and put a comma where it belongs.

1. On a rainy day in May Sally left for Texas.
2. For the first time in years Chuck took a vacation.
3. According to last month's statement one check bounced.
4. To all the grandmas in the world I sing this song.
5. In the name of my fellow workers I accept this award.
6. While walking in the park I found a penny.
7. Before she runs she always stretches.
8. When he studies Bob listens to music.
9. After running the race her legs felt tired.
10. Once in a while I like to eat ice cream.

B. How do you know where a sentence should be divided? It often helps to read the sentence out loud. Then you can hear two separate groups of words. Read aloud the example below. Notice how you pause at the comma.

> Although she had met Matt before, Kim didn't remember him.

Read and copy each sentence. Underline the first word group at the beginning of the sentence. Put a comma where it belongs.

1. As she was sewing the curtains Suzie hummed.
2. While you were sleeping I was out working.
3. After the men delivered the desk Don painted it.
4. Because you are my friend I'll do this for you.
5. Whenever I hear that song I feel like crying.

C. Most very short sentences do not need a comma. They are made up of just one group of words. Some short sentences, however, are made of two different word groups. To show a pause, a comma must be used.

> When Joe was younger, he ran very fast.

> However, now Joe can run longer distances.

Read the sentences aloud. Rewrite the sentences adding a comma to show a pause.

Reminder

Write your sentences on a separate sheet of paper.

1. Wait a minute he's over there.
2. Your shirt is torn I think.
3. If you go I will stay.
4. When spring comes flowers bloom.
5. Will Jay be home soon or not?
6. To be honest I don't know.
7. In fact your idea makes sense.
8. On the swim team Gail breaks every record.
9. Usually the mail comes before noon.
10. On nice days he walks to work.

Lesson 5 Commas in a Series

Words to Know

series three or more words or groups of words in a row

comma (,) a punctuation mark that tells when to pause between words or word groups

The word *series* sounds like SEER-eez.

Sometimes a sentence gives a list of things, people, places, or ideas. These words or groups of words will appear in a **series**. A series is a list of three or more words or word groups in a row.

A. **Commas** are used to separate the things, people, places, or ideas in the series from one another. Look at the examples:

words in a series ⟶ apples, oranges, and bananas

word groups in a series ⟶ out the door, down the driveway, and up the hill

Using commas to separate words in a series makes the meaning clearer. Without commas, the words would run together. Do not use a comma after the last word in the series.

correct ⟶ Jack bought eggs, sausage, and bread for breakfast.

incorrect ⟶ Jack bought eggs, sausage, and bread, for breakfast.

Read and copy the sentences. Underline the words in each series. Put the commas where they belong.

1. The Joads were sad broke and hungry.
2. Tim Carl and Kate came into the kitchen.
3. Please don't ever lie cheat or steal.
4. We spent all day reading writing and studying.
5. The pets for sale include fish birds dogs and cats.
6. Set the table with knives forks and spoons.

B.   Commas are also used to separate groups of words in a series. Do not use a comma after the last word group in the series.

correct ⟶ We need to make our plans, buy our tickets, and pack our suitcases before we leave.

incorrect ⟶ We need to make our plans, buy our tickets, and pack our suitcases, before we leave.

Read and copy the sentences. Underline the word groups in each series. Put the commas where they belong.

1. Over the log under the tree and through the woods ran the wolf.
2. The birds found a safe place looked for some straw and built a nest.
3. Tell me where you're going who is going with you and when you'll be home.
4. We will fish in the river swim in the lake and sleep under the stars when we go camping.
5. I take a bath brush my teeth and comb my hair when I get up.
6. My brother will mow the grass paint his room and clean the car on Saturday.

C.   Do not mix different kinds of words or word groups in a series. If the series lists words, each thing should be a word. If the series lists word groups, each thing should be a word group.

correct ⟶ His new shirt is white, blue, and yellow.

incorrect ⟶ His new shirt is white, blue, and it has a little yellow in it, too.

Read the sentences. Notice that the things in each series are not the same. Rewrite each underlined series. Use all words or all word groups in each series.

1. This recipe calls for <u>flour, sugar, and I need some vanilla.</u>
2. I wouldn't do that <u>for love, for money, or even if you gave me a free trip.</u>
3. Sheila got <u>a haircut, a coloring, and treated herself to a manicure.</u>
4. Joe likes <u>fishing, to laugh, and root beer.</u>
5. For lunch we will eat <u>chicken, potatoes, and we'll have pie.</u>
6. Some dogs will <u>jump, bark and they will bite when they are mad.</u>

Lesson 6   Commas That Set Off Words

Words to Know

set off to separate one part of a sentence from another part

introductory words words that begin a sentence

noun of address a person's name used when speaking directly to that person

Some sentences have parts at that can be separated from the rest of the sentence. These words are separated or **set off** from other words using commas. The part might be at the beginning, middle, or end.

A. Words that begin a sentence with a thought and a pause are called **introductory words**. A comma is often used to set off introductory words from the rest of the sentence.

> **Yes,** June was told about the test. **In fact,** I told her myself.
>
> ← introductory words →

In speaking, you would pause after the introductory words. In writing, you follow these words with a comma.

Reminder

When should you use a comma? Try reading the sentence aloud. If you don't need to pause, you don't need to use a comma.

comma needed ⟶ Before you attend class, you have to enroll.

comma not needed ⟶ Then the frogs croaked loudly.

Read and copy each sentence. Underline the introductory word or word groups. If a comma is needed, put the comma where it belongs.

1. By this time next year Ben will be back home.
2. Then the rain stopped as suddenly as it had begun.
3. If you list the names in order they will be easier to find.

B. Sometimes a group of words is used to explain another word. These words may be in the middle of the sentence. Use commas to set off this group of words.

> Dr. Stevens, **our family dentist,** works four days a week.

Rewrite each sentence. Use commas where they are needed.

1. Aunt Mary my mother's sister lives in New York.
2. Puff my long-haired cat is white and black.
3. That tree which I planted myself is ten years old.
4. Our home a four-bedroom house has a pool.

C. Sometimes a word or group of words breaks up the thought of a sentence. These could be in the middle, too. Use commas to set off this word group from the rest of the sentence.

Wanda tried, **I am sure,** to do the right thing.

Read the sentences. Choose a group of words from the box to complete each sentence. Add commas as needed.

I hope	most likely	it seems	I suppose

1. You will _____ want to study tonight.
2. The movie _____ will be over soon.
3. This money should _____ be enough.
4. The race _____ will start soon.

D. When you speak to someone, you often use his or her name. In a written sentence, this is called the **noun of address**. This name is set off with one or more commas.

John, please pass the salt.

noun of address

If the sentence begins with a name, set it off with a comma. If the name is in the middle of the sentence, use commas before and after it. If the sentence ends with a name, set it off with a comma.

begins with name ⟶ **Jean,** please help me.

name in middle ⟶ Please, **Jean,** help me.

ends with name ⟶ Please help me, **Jean.**

Rewrite each sentence. Put one or more commas where they belong.

1. Karen what is your favorite movie?
2. I think Justine that it is *The Wizard of Oz*.
3. Who played the Tin Man in that movie Anthony?
4. I don't know Mary but Judy Garland played Dorothy.

Lesson 7   Direct Quotations

Words to Know

quotation a sentence that shows what someone has said

quotation marks (" ") the punctuation marks used to set off a direct quotation

direct quotation the exact words a person said

indirect quotation what a person said, but not in the speaker's exact words

The word *quotation* sounds like kwoh-TAY-shuhn.

Sometimes a sentence tells what a person has said. This is called a **quotation**. Quotations can be written exactly like what someone said. A quotation also can be about what someone said but not in the speaker's exact words.

A. There are two kind of quotations: direct and indirect. A **direct quotation** means you that you are reading a person's exact words.

Quotation marks are a kind of punctuation that marks the beginning and end of a quotation. Quotation marks in a sentence tell you that you are reading exactly what a person said. The first word in a direct quotation begins with a capital letter.

direct quotation ⟶ **"Let's go,"** said Sam.

quotation marks

If there are no quotation marks, the words are not exactly what the person said. This kind of quotation is called an **indirect quotation**. You do not use quotation marks with an indirect quotation.

indirect quotation ⟶ Sam said we should go.

Read each sentence. Decide if it includes a direct quotation or if the sentence is an indirect quotation. Write *direct* or *indirect* as an answer for each number.

1. "Where's my hat?" Frank asked.
2. Judy told us we should call the office.
3. Angela said that she'd be late.
4. Edward asked, "How much does that cost?"

B. Use a comma to separate a direct quotation from the rest of the sentence. Look carefully at these examples. Notice where the commas are used.

Mrs. Green said, "Annie is not home right now."

"I'm sorry I missed her," Stuart replied.

Read each sentence. Rewrite it adding the correct punctuation. Use quotation marks and commas.

1. Walt asked Where is my umbrella?
2. Three students are absent today said the teacher.
3. I bought a red sports car John said happily.
4. Jason shouted Where is my jacket?
5. What is your real name? Chuck asked
6. Meg answered My real name is Margaret.
7. Fred asked Is that right?
8. I thought you were lost! Charlie shouted

C. Sometimes a direct quotation is broken into two parts. Use quotation marks before and after each part. Use commas to set off each part from the rest of the sentence.

capital letter   small letter

"If only," the football coach groaned, "we had made one more touchdown."

You know the first word in a direct quotation begins with a capital letter. When a quotation is broken into two parts, the second part begins with a small letter.

Read each sentence. Rewrite it using the correct punctuation.

1. My mother he said will be here soon.
2. If we were rich said Sam we'd help the poor.
3. Those who need shots the doctor said can wait here.

Lesson 8   Dates and Place Names

complete date a date that shows month, day, and year

place name name of a place that has two or more words such as a city and its state or country

Punctuation marks are important in complete dates and place names. A **complete date** shows the month, day, and year. A **place name** is the name of a place that has two or more words to describe it. Without commas and periods, the different parts of dates and place names would run together.

> complete date ⟶ June 6, 1944
>
> place name ⟶ Paris, France

A.   In a complete date, always use a comma between the day and the year. Use another comma if the date does not appear at the end of a sentence. Place the second comma after the year.

School started on September 9, 1996.

The baby was born on May 5, 1996, a Sunday.

Rewrite each sentence. Add commas as needed.
1. Marty gave a party on July 4 1996.
2. On January 2 1996 my uncle got married.
3. This tree was planted on April 18 1996 by Betty.
4. The old soldier was born on May 10 1920.
5. Before March 15 1989 my family lived in Mexico.
6. My birthday is February 9 1980.

B.   Do not use a comma when only the month and the year appear.

April 1865

January 1998

Read each sentence. Notice the punctuation of dates. Find each error and write the date correctly.

1. Did you see the Winter Olympics in February, 1994?
2. The games began on February 12 1994.
3. John F. Kennedy was born on May 29 1917.
4. In November, 1963, he died.
5. On December 11 1941 the U.S. went to war.
6. World War II ended on August 15 1945.

C. A place name tells the city and state or the city and country of a place. Look at the map below. It shows the states of Kansas, Missouri, Oklahoma, and Arkansas.

Each of the cities on the map has a place name. A place name gives the city first and state or country second. Always use a comma between the name of the city and the name of the state or country it is in.

She wants to visit Kansas City, Missouri.

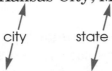

city   state

He lives in Little Rock, Arkansas.

If the place name does not end the sentence, use another comma. Place the second comma after the name of the state or country.

Lucy needs to go to St. Louis, Missouri, on business.

Oklahoma City, Oklahoma, is having a homecoming parade.

Read the place names in each sentence. Rewrite the sentences. Put the commas in the right places.

1. He wants to visit London England.
2. Marlene is going to Madrid Spain in January.
3. I would like to visit San Francisco California in the fall.
4. I would go to Phoenix Arizona if the weather were nice.
5. Sue took a bus to Baltimore Maryland.
6. Bill wants to travel to Sidney Australia on an airplane.

Lesson 9 Colons, Semicolons, and Hyphens

Words to Know

colon (:) a punctuation mark used to show that a list or an example will follow

semicolon (;) a punctuation mark that shows a long pause but not an end to a sentence

hyphen (-) a punctuation mark used to join words together

Colons, semicolons, and hyphens are very useful marks of punctuation. They help make your writing easier to read.

The word *colon* sounds like KOH-luhn.

A. A **colon (:)** is written as two dots one on top of the other. A colon shows that a list is coming in the same sentence. Use a colon just before the list.

Bring the following things: **socks, toothbrush, shampoo**.

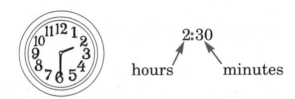

colon   list

Read each sentence. Find the two words in each sentence that should have a colon between them. Write those words adding the colon between.

1. I will invite these people Jon, Bob, and Sal.
2. Bill likes these sports soccer, basketball, and baseball.
3. Lisa collects three kinds of music jazz, classical, and rock.

B. To write the time, use a colon between numbers showing hours and minutes. Look at the clock and time below.

2:30

hours   minutes

Look at the times on each clock. Write the time using a colon.

1.   2.   3.

C. When you write a letter, it begins with a greeting. There are two kinds of letters: business and friendly. Use a colon after the greeting in a business letter. Use a comma after the greeting in a friendly letter.

> **business greeting** —→ Dear Dr. Bones:

> **friendly greeting** —→ Dear Aunt June,

Rewrite each letter greeting. Write *friendly* or *business* next to each. Write the correct punctuation.

1. Dear Sir or Madam
2. Dear Grandpa
3. Dear Mr. Granger
4. Attention Dr. Bones
5. My dearest Theresa
6. To whom it may concern

D. Use a **semicolon** to show a strong pause in thought. A semicolon shows a stronger pause than a comma does. It shows a weaker pause than a period does. A semicolon can join two sentences that are close in thought. A semicolon can separate things in a series if there is other punctuation.

Reminder

A pause in thought means to slow down but not stop.

> It was a crisp autumn day; it was perfect weather for a hike.

> We drove to Chicago, Illinois; Detroit, Michigan; and Ames, Iowa.

Use a semicolon to join two sentences. Use a semicolon to separate things in a series. Write your new sentences.

1. Richard liked to fish. He fished all day.
2. I went to Paris, France, Athens, Greece and Rome, Italy.
3. Jan swam in record time. She won the medal.
4. It was almost time to go. They ran to the bus.

E. **Hyphens** are a punctuation mark used to join words together into one word. For example, hyphens are used to write numbers 21 to 99 and fractions less than one.

The word *hyphen* sounds like HEYE-fuhn.

> **numbers** —→ twenty-one   one hundred ninety-nine

> **fractions** —→ one-third   two and one-half

Some words in each sentence need a hyphen. Find the words that must be joined. Write the corrected words.

1. Jo will be twenty four soon.
2. Rod's aunt is almost ninety two.
3. I need four and one half pounds of fish.
4. There are two hundred sixty three students graduating.

Lesson 10 | What Is a Noun?

Words to Know

noun part of speech that names a person, place, thing, event, or idea

common noun a word that names any person, place, thing, event, or idea

Words that name are called nouns. A **noun** may name a person (firefighter) or a place (fire station). A noun may name an event (forest fire) or an idea (bravery).

A. Nouns like *boy* and *city* are used to talk about any boy or any city. These are **common nouns**. They begin with lowercase, or small, letters.

common nouns ⟶ girl sock concert happiness

Read the words listed below. Find and list the common nouns. You should be able to find 14 of them.

leaf	bird	the	pretty	sister
a	bed	have	our	seen
for	fox	its	hill	tired
peanut	too	ticket	so	morning
fun	smaller	cake	table	run
away	baker	also	ant	very

B. Words like *clown*, *doctor*, and *aunt* are common nouns that name people. Words like *park*, *mountain*, and *town* are common nouns that name places. Look at the nouns in the sentences below.

name people ⟶ The **nurse** is very nice. She is helping a **patient**.

name places ⟶ The **hospital** is very large. It faces the **river**.

Rewrite each sentence. Circle the common nouns. Then write what that noun names: person or place.

1. Run down the hill with me.

2. That clerk is new here.
3. Our home is neat and clean.
4. May I call your office?
5. The janitor is working late.

C.

Words like *computer*, *candy bar*, and *hat* are nouns that name things. Words like *contest*, *party*, and *trial* are nouns that name events. Look at the nouns in the sentences below.

name things ⟶ I wrapped the **present** carefully.
The **dishes** inside seemed fragile.

name events ⟶ I walked to the **party**. It was for Tim's **birthday**.

Rewrite each sentence. Circle the common nouns. Then write what that noun names: *thing* or *event*.

1. Those pencils are new.
2. The concert started too late.
3. The race was very exciting.
4. His truck is old and rusty.
5. Who will loan me a dollar?

D.

Many nouns are one word. Some nouns are made up of two or more words. The words in these nouns make sense as a group. The noun *alarm clock*, for example, has a different meaning than the separate nouns *alarm* and *clock*.

two word nouns ⟶ ice cream   high school

Rewrite the sentences. Circle the nouns that are made of two words.

1. Jack hit a home run.
2. Rosa caught the fly ball.
3. Bert bought a new garbage can.
4. The fire truck arrived just in time.

E.

Sometimes a noun is made of two or more words joined by hyphens.

nouns with hyphens ⟶ mother-in-law   mayor-elect

Reminder

A hyphen is a punctuation mark made from a dash (-).

Rewrite the sentences. Circle the nouns made of two or more words.

1. Mary's great-grandson sent her flowers.
2. Jean was the maid-of-honor at my wedding.
3. Her sister-in-law caught the bouquet.
4. Joe's great-grandfather danced with the bride.

Lesson 11 Proper Nouns

proper noun a word that names a *specific* person, place, thing, event, or idea

common noun a word that names *any* person, place, thing, event, or idea

You use **proper nouns** every day. The name of every person in your family is a proper noun. So are the names of your city and state.

Reminder

A common noun begins with a lower case letter: woman, state, event.

A. Everything that can be named with a **proper noun** can also be named with a **common noun**.

proper noun ⟶ Mars

common noun ⟶ planet

Choose the proper noun in each pair and write it on your paper.

1. student   Alice
2. Hawaii   state
3. city   Austin
4. pet   Fluffy
5. Labor Day   holiday

B. Like common nouns, proper nouns can be made up of more than one word.

proper nouns ⟶ South Dakota, Edgar Allan Poe, Rose Bowl

Read each sentence. Rewrite only the proper nouns.

1. Did you invite Andrew to the party?
2. Do you mean Andrew Carlton or Andrew Rosenberg?
3. We bought the birthday cake at Ramona Pastry Shop.
4. The party will be held at Central Park.
5. We got the decorations at Fun Town.

C. Every proper noun is the particular name of a common noun.

common noun ——→ park

proper noun ——→ Central Park

Match the common nouns from List 1 with their proper nouns in List 2. Write both nouns together on your paper.

List 1	**List 2**
1. river	a. Dr. Joyce Brothers
2. school	b. Muir Woods
3. doctor	c. Mississippi River
4. forest	d. Carlmont High School

D. Names or titles of particular things are proper nouns. Proper nouns are always capitalized. Sometimes a short word is part of a name or title. These short words are not capitalized. Only the important words in a name or title are capitalized.

names or titles ——→ Washington High School
American Legion
James and the Giant Peach

Reminder

To *capitalize* a word means to begin it with a capital letter.

Rewrite each sentence. Capitalize the important words in the names and titles that are underlined.

1. The name of that company is <u>donna white and daughters</u>.
2. We visited the <u>tower of london</u> during our trip.
3. Linda wrote a book report on <u>huckleberry finn</u>.
4. Tom lives near the <u>university of california at los angeles</u>.
5. The best store for food is <u>big bear supermarket</u>.

E. Remember that a common noun does *not* begin with a capital letter.

Read the sentences. Are there proper nouns that should be capitalized? Are there common nouns that should not be capitalized? Rewrite the sentences correctly.

1. I live at the Corner of polk street and tenth avenue.
2. He is the Catcher for the georgia bulldogs baseball team.
3. She had Lunch at north beach pizza parlor.
4. We took the Train to north station.

Lesson 12 Regular Plural Nouns

Words to Know

singular noun a word that names just one person, place, thing, event, or idea

regular plural noun a word that ends in *-s* or *-es* and names more than one person, place, thing, event, or idea

Most nouns have two forms, *singular* and *plural*. **Singular nouns** name one person, place, or thing. Plural nouns name more than one.

A. Many **regular plural nouns** are formed by adding *-s* to singular nouns.

> desk/desks   plant/plants   home/homes   dog/dogs

Read each word in the list. Rewrite the regular plural nouns. You should be able to find 15 of them.

books	race	birthdays	cars
minutes	corners	legs	skate
gardens	clocks	listen	oranges
boats	sisters	fast	noises
lines	airplanes	coats	skin

B. Some singular nouns end in *s, ss, sh, ch, x,* or *z.* The plural of these nouns is formed by adding *es*.

> bus/buses   kiss/kisses   dish/dishes   patch/patches
>
> fox/foxes   buzz/buzzes

Read each word. Write the plural form.

1. guess   2. tax
3. buzz   4. match
5. bunch   6. flash

C. Not all words that end in *s* are plural nouns. Many words of all kinds end in *s*.

has   bus   yes   us

Read the words in the list below. Rewrite only the regular plural nouns.

gifts   kiss   crows
cross   was   windows

D. A singular noun names only one thing. A plural noun can name any number of things–two, twenty, a hundred, a thousand, or more. To name more than one thing, use a plural noun.

one apple

three **trees**

a bunch of **carrots**

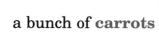

Look at the singular nouns. Write the plural form.

1. bird   2. tree   3. apple
4. car   5. radio   6. book

Lesson 13 Irregular Plural Nouns

Words to Know

irregular not usual

irregular plural noun a noun that does not form the plural by just adding -s or -es

consonants all letters of the alphabet that are not vowels

The word **irregular** means "not usual." A noun that does not form the plural by just adding -s or -es is an **irregular plural noun**. Some irregular plural nouns follow rules and some do not. Use a dictionary if you need help.

A. Some singular nouns end in *f.* In most cases, you will form the plural by changing the *f* to *v* and adding -es. Some singular nouns end in *fe.* In most cases, you will form the plural by changing the *fe* to *ve* and adding -s.

half/halves   knife/knives

Match the singular noun in the first column with its plural form in the second column. Write both together.

Reminder

Write your word pairs on a separate piece of paper.

Singular Nouns	Plural Nouns
1. calf	thieves
2. leaf	knives
3. loaf	calves
4. thief	wives
5. knife	leaves
6. wife	lives
7. life	loaves

B. Some singular nouns that end in *f* and *fe* do *not* follow the rules. These nouns need only an -s to be made plural. Look in a dictionary if you are not sure of the spelling.

chef/chefs   safe/safes

Read each sentence. Look at the underlined noun. Write the plural form of the noun from the box.

chiefs	staffs	roofs	beliefs

1. My belief in your talent is still strong.
2. The chief was glad to see us.
3. Our old roof needs new tiles.
4. The school staff has the day off.

C. Singular nouns that end in *y* follow two rules. Does a vowel come before the *y*? If so, add -*s*. Does a **consonant** come before the *y*? If so, change the *y* to *i* and add -*es*.

The word *consonant* sounds like KAHN-suh-nuhnt.

bay/bay**s**   party/part**ies**

Read each sentence. Choose the plural form of each underlined noun from the box. Rewrite the sentences with the correct plural noun.

libraries	toys	activities	keys	spies	trays

1. Brad has too many toy.
2. Kari visited two library today.
3. Lisa has six key on her key ring.
4. Tina likes after-school activity.
5. We got your name from three spy.
6. The bus boy cleaned off all the tray.

D. Some nouns stay the same whether they are singular or plural.

one deer/two deer   one fish/two fish

Choose the plural noun from the box that completes each sentence. Rewrite your sentences correctly.

moose	fish	pair	sheep	deer

1. First I saw one sheep, and then I saw many _____.
2. One big moose walked ahead of the other ten _____.
3. I bought and extra pair of socks. Now I have two _____.
4. The red fish swam in a school of _____.
5. I saw one deer in the yard. Later there were many _____.

Lesson 14   Possessive Nouns

Words to Know

possessive noun a noun that shows ownership or relationship

apostrophe (') the punctuation mark used to form possessive nouns and other word forms

The **possessive noun** is very useful. Without it, you would have to use more words to say the same thing. "This is the garden of my grandmother" is hard to say. "This is my grandmother's garden" is much easier.

The word *apostrophe* sounds like uh-PAWS-truh-fee.

A. To form the possessive of most singular nouns, add an **apostrophe** and an *-s*.

> the child**'s** uncle   an owner**'s** manual

Read each pair of sentences. Look at the underlined noun. Write the sentences using the possessive form of the underlined noun in the blank.

1. The hat belongs to <u>Anna</u>. It is ____ hat.
2. <u>Byron</u> bought a bowling ball. That is ____ bowling ball.
3. <u>Kevin</u> caught a trout. Dad will cook ____ trout for dinner.
4. My <u>sister</u> loaned me her scarf. Do you like my ____ scarf?
5. Our <u>group</u> wrote a report. Our ____ report was the best one of all.

B. Some singular nouns end in *s*. Usually, the possessive is formed by adding an apostrophe and an *-s*.

> Aunt Gladys**'s** idea   the hostess**'s** sweater

Read each group of words. Notice the noun in parentheses. Write the singular possessive form of that noun. The first example is done for you.

1. the (class) plans
   the class's plans
2. the (dress) zipper
3. my friend (Jess) homework
4. young (Boris) summer schedule
5. the (bass) mouth
6. Mr. (Jones) car

C.   Most plural nouns end in *-s*. It is easy to form the possessive of these nouns. Simply add an apostrophe.

     the books' covers   the boys' locker room

Read the sentences and the plural nouns in parentheses. Write each sentence using possessive plural nouns for each. The first example is done for you.

1. The (houses) yards were neat.
   The houses' yards were neat.
2. The three (cousins) shirts were the same color.
3. Many (artists) paintings covered the walls.
4. Four (dogs) howls filled the air.
5. The (babies) rattles were broken.
6. All the (teachers) classes left early.
7. Many of the (girls) shoes are too small.

D.   Some plural nouns do not end in *s*. The possessive form of these nouns is made by adding an apostrophe and an *-s*.

     the children**'s** hour   the women**'s** shoes

Look at the pictures. Choose the possessive plural noun from the box to match each picture. Write a sentence using your choice.

the men's conversation   the oxen's cart   the sheep's wool

1.

2.

3.

Lesson 15 Personal Pronouns

Words to Know

personal pronoun a word that takes the place of a certain person or thing

subjective pronoun a personal pronoun that *performs* an action

objective pronoun a personal pronoun that *receives* an action

antecedent the noun or group of nouns that a pronoun replaces

All nouns can be replaced by pronouns.

 A. Most **personal pronouns** have two forms.

I/me   he/him   she/her   they/them   we/us

Only two personal pronouns do not change form.

it/it   you/you

How do you know which form to use? Think about how the pronoun will be used in a sentence. A **subjective pronoun** usually *performs* an action. An **objective pronoun** usually *receives* an action.

subjective pronoun ⟶ **He** plays with the dog.

objective pronoun ⟶ The dog plays with **him**.

Read the sentences and the pairs of pronouns in parentheses. Rewrite each sentence with the correct pronoun.

1. (He, Him) built a beautiful bookcase.
2. The class gave some roses to (she, her).
3. That big gift is for (I, me).
4. (They, Them) already met the new neighbors.
5. (We, Us) asked for a second chance.

B. A personal pronoun can take the place of a noun or a group of nouns.

Gloria told Mary the news. ⟶ Gloria told **her** the news.

Read the sentences. Replace the underlined nouns with pronouns from the box. Rewrite the sentences using the pronouns. You may use words more than once.

us	she	it	them	they	he

1. Manny told <u>Jim and Pat</u> the news.
2. Kim made <u>a necklace</u> for Sandy.
3. <u>Dr. Sue Kelly</u> has an office next door.
4. Annie gave <u>the prizes</u> to Matt and me.

C.   The **antecedent** is the noun or group of nouns that a pronoun replaces. In the example below, the noun *building* is the antecedent of the pronoun *it*.

That **building** is tall.   **It** is ten stories high.

The word *antecedent* sounds like AN-tuh-cee-duhnt.

Find the pronoun in each sentence. Write the pronoun and its antecedent. The first one is done for you.

1. When the flowers bloom, Sal will pick them.
   them ⟶ *flowers*
2. Robert told the children to follow him.
3. Find the book and give it to Joe.
4. Sharon will sing if Mark asks her.
5. Pam and Sandy know they must hurry.

Reminder

Copy the sentences and show your work on a separate paper.

D.   A pronoun must *agree with* its antecedent. To "agree with" means to be the same in person and number.

agree in person ⟶ As **customers** enter, **they** take a number.

disagree in person ⟶ As **customers** enter, <u>you</u> take a number.

agree in number ⟶ Wash **one** apple and eat **it**.

disagree in number ⟶ Wash one apple and eat <u>them</u>.

Read the sentences. Notice that the underlined pronouns and their antecedents do not agree. Replace the underlined pronouns to correct the sentences. Rewrite the sentences correctly.

1. Toast two slices of bread and butter <u>it</u>.
2. Tim thought that <u>they</u> smelled a gas leak.
3. Ben asked Sarah what <u>they</u> wanted for lunch.
4. All good dancers practice whenever <u>she</u> can.

Lesson 16 Reflexive Pronouns

Words to Know

reflexive pronoun a pronoun that refers back to a noun or pronoun in the same sentence

A **reflexive pronoun** refers to a noun or pronoun in the same sentence. It is used in two ways. In some sentences a reflexive pronoun adds more information. In other sentences, a reflexive pronoun adds more importance to another word.

adds information ⟶ Freddie built a house for **himself**.

adds importance ⟶ Freddie **himself** did all the work.

A. Reflexive pronouns are easy to spot. They always end with -*self* or -*selves*.

Read the list of words. Find the reflexive pronouns. You should be able to find eight.

everyone	herself	yourselves
myself	selfish	nobody
themselves	yourself	himself
ourselves	itself	someone

B. Reflexive pronouns must agree with their antecedents in number. A plural antecedent needs a plural reflexive pronoun.

The **players** were proud of **themselves**.

A singular antecedent needs a singular reflexive pronoun.

Coach Megan Brown ordered cocoa for **herself**.

Reminder

The *antecedent* is the word or group of words that a pronoun replaces.
"To agree with" means to be the same in person and number.

Look at the pictures below. Choose the word that describes what each picture shows. Then choose the reflexive pronoun from the box that agrees with that word. The first one is done for you.

itself	themselves	herself	himself

1.

football, footballs
football + itself

2.

girl, girls

3.

man, men

4.

woman, women

C. Suppose you want to talk about yourself or a group that you belong to. There are two reflexive pronouns that you could use: *myself* and *ourselves*.

you alone ⟶ I painted the fence **myself**.

you and others ⟶ We found **ourselves** lost in the forest.

Read the sentences. Use *myself* or *ourselves* to complete each sentence.

1. I ____ pulled all those weeds.
2. Jane and I felt sorry for ____.
3. Living by ____ makes me lonely sometimes.
4. All of us need to respect ____.
5. When I dropped the box, I hurt ____.

Reminder

Write the complete sentences on your paper.

D. Suppose you are talking *directly* to one or more people. There are two reflexive pronouns that you can use: *yourself* or *yourselves*.

Use *yourself* or *yourselves* to complete each sentence.

1. You children need to wash ____.
2. You, Rudy, should stand up for ____.
3. Today, you and Marty must work by ____.
4. Solve the problem ____, Leo.

Lesson 17 Possessive Pronouns

possessive pronoun a pronoun that shows ownership or relationship

Possessive pronouns make it easier to speak and write. Without possessive pronouns, you would have to say: "The cat owned by me hid under the desk belonging to me." It is much easier to say, "**My** cat hid under **my** desk."

A. Some possessive pronouns come right before nouns: **my** friend. Sometimes other words come between the pronoun and the noun: **my** best friend.

POSSESSIVE PRONOUNS USED BEFORE NOUNS	
Singular	**Plural**
my	our
your	your
his, her, its	their

Look at the pictures. Read the sentences and the pronouns in parentheses. Rewrite each sentence with the correct possessive pronoun.

1. The hat is on (her, hers) head.
2. Sean is (their, theirs) son.
3. (Mine, My) bike has a flat tire.
4. Can I borrow (your, yours) pump?

B. Some possessive pronouns can stand alone in a sentence.

The flowers are **yours**.   That car is **hers**.

Read the pronouns in the chart below.

Singular	Plural
mine	ours
yours	yours
his, hers, its	theirs

Read the pairs of sentences and the pronouns that follow. Decide which pronoun can stand alone. Write each sentence correctly. You will use both pronouns—one in each sentence.

1. This is ____ library card. This library card is ____.
   (my, mine)
2. This picnic lunch is ____. Fred and I packed ____ picnic lunch. (our, ours)
3. I heard that you lost ____ pen. Is this pen ____?
   (your, yours)
4. Sarah walked to ____ house. Is the red house ____?
   (hers, her)

C. Remember that possessive pronouns must agree with their antecedents. Read the example. Notice that the underlined word is the antecedent.

Have <u>you</u> eaten **your** breakfast?

The <u>brothers</u> shared a room. **Their** room was very neat.

Read the sentences and the words in parentheses. Rewrite each sentence with the possessive pronoun that agrees with the underlined word or words.

1. My <u>father</u> enjoys working in (his, her) garden.
2. <u>Sally</u> pointed out (mine, her) favorite building.
3. <u>I</u> am sure of (theirs, my) feelings.
4. <u>Paul and Jan</u> cooked (my, their) own dinner.
5. <u>Don and I</u> discussed (its, our) problems.
6. The <u>women</u> had (their, her) meeting in the den.
7. My <u>uncle</u> showed me (his, our) latest drawings.

Lesson 18   Indefinite Pronouns

Words to Know

indefinite pronoun a pronoun that stands for a noun that is not known

antecedent the noun or group of nouns that a pronoun replaces

The word *indefinite* sounds like ihn-DEHF-uh-niht.

You know that a pronoun must agree with the noun it replaces. But you can't always tell what noun is being replaced. Use an **indefinite pronoun** when the antecedent is not known.

    I wonder why **nobody** is answering the phone.

A. Indefinite pronouns are not exact. They refer to a general group rather than to a known **antecedent**.

Read the sentences. What pronouns stand for nouns that are not known? Write the indefinite pronouns. The first example is done for you.

1. We had thought of everything.
   everything
2. Nothing had been left to chance.
3. Anybody can come to the lecture.
4. Everyone is welcome.
5. Someone thought a mistake had been made.
6. Nobody could figure out the problem.
7. Bill bought one of each.
8. Either will work.
9. May I have another, please?
10. Bring both with you tomorrow.

B. You might not know the antecedent of an indefinite pronoun. But sometimes you can tell whether it is singular or plural. Look at the indefinite pronouns in the box. They are used for *singular* antecedents.

another	anybody	anyone	anything
each	either	everybody	everyone
everything	neither	nobody	no one
nothing	one	other	somebody
someone	something		

Choose a pronoun from the box as you rewrite each sentence.

1. Both choices are dangerous. ____ is safe.
2. ____ went home early.
3. We heard ____ coming up the stairs.
4. The doctor did ____ she could.
5. The patient was willing to try ____.
6. Gary spilled ____ on his shirt.
7. ____ was at the good-bye party.
8. ____ will be enough for the three of us.
9. Does ____ know the answer to this question?
10. ____ is ripe yet.

C. Some indefinite pronouns replace only *plural* antecedents.

Four boys came to the meeting. **All** of them were late.

both	all	several	many	few

Choose a pronoun from the box as you rewrite each sentence.

1. Janet and Lisa arrived early. ____ of them were wearing red shoes.
2. Only a ____ of the students know the answer.
3. Prizes were given to ____ contestants but not all of them.
4. We have ____ good ideas for fixing up this room.
5. LaToya had a lot of homework. She did not finish ____ of it.
6. The horses are waiting at the fence. ____ want carrots.
7. ____ hope to climb the mountain. ____ actually do it.
8. Max is collecting stamps. He already has ____ that his grandfather gave him.

Lesson 19

Interrogative and Demonstrative Pronouns

Words to Know

interrogative pronoun a pronoun used to ask a question
demonstrative pronoun a pronoun that points out nouns or other pronouns

The word *interrogative* sounds like in-tuh-RAWG-uh-tihv.

An **interrogative pronoun** is used in sentences that ask a question.

What is on your mind?

A. All interrogative pronouns start with the letters *wh*. The interrogative pronouns used most often are **who, whom, whose, which,** and **what**

Read the sentences below. Write the interrogative pronoun in each sentence.
1. Who is knocking at the door?
2. Of all your hats, which is your favorite?
3. Of all their cars, whose will win the race?
4. To whom does this puppy belong?
5. What can you mean by that?

B. Interrogative pronouns have different uses. Study this list of rules.
- *Who* and *whom* refer to a person or persons.

    Who are you? To **whom** are you speaking?

    Use *who* for subjective pronouns. Use *whom* for objective pronouns.
- *Whose* is used to ask about ownership or relationship.

    Whose is this?

- *What* refers to things, places, and ideas.

    What do you mean?

- *Which* is used when there is a choice.

    Which of these do you like better?

Read each pair of sentences. Choose *who, whom, whose, what,* or *which* to complete the second sentence in each pair.

1. This hat belongs to Jane. ____ is that one? (whose, who)
2. I have pink dishes and gold-trimmed dishes. Of the two sets, ____ makes the food look better? (whom, which)
3. Howard really likes baseball. ____ is Betty's favorite sport? (What, Who)
4. The roses are for Jane. For ____ are the carnations? (which, whom)
5. Dan visits Gordon. ____ will visit Angie? (Who, What)

C.   There are only four **demonstrative pronouns**. They are **this, that, these,** and **those. This** and **that** are singular. **These** and **those** are plural.

The word *demonstrative* sounds like dih-MAWN-struh-tihv.

Read the sentences. Write the demonstrative pronoun in each sentence. Tell if the pronoun is singular or plural. The first one is done for you

1. Is this your house?   *this – singular*
2. No, that is my house, over there.
3. Those are my sister's shoes.
4. My brother's shoes are these, right here.

D.   **This** and **these** refer to things that are near. **That** and **those** refer to things that are farther away.

    I like **this** one better than **that** one over there.

Imagine you are the person in the picture below. How would you complete each sentence? Rewrite the sentences, choosing the correct demonstrative pronouns.

1. I like (this, that) puppy.
2. (This, That) horse belongs to Mr. Jones.
3. Look at (these, those) cute puppies.
4. The horse stays under (these, those) trees.

Lesson 20 | What Is a Verb?

Word to Know

verb the part of speech that expresses action or being

Most **verbs** are action words. Verbs express or show action. These verbs are easy to recognize. Just try to act them out. If you can perform the action, the word is a verb.

action verbs ⟶ drive, sing, dance, jump

A. Think about words like *hop* and *skip*. Can you act them out? If so, you know that they are verbs.

Read each word listed below. Write the verbs that show action. You should be able to find 20 verbs.

Reminder

Write your list on a separate sheet of paper. Title your list "Verbs".

whistle	work	until	ourselves	pretty
rabbit	one	rub	shake	seven
read	robin	quite	save	cry
city	climb	good	go	fly
dig	girl	food	eat	drink
funny	laugh	lift	for	into
ride	the	apple	listen	buy
toss	pumpkin	leaf	catch	quickly

B. Verbs are very important words. You could not tell a story without using verbs. You could not write even one sentence without using a verb. In fact, this whole book is filled with verbs.

Read the directions. **Answer** the questions carefully. This book **helps** you with sentences.

Rewrite the story below. Complete each sentence with a verb from the box.

plays	brushes	talks	opens
combs	laughs	jogs	waits
eats	washes	walks	

Every morning, Steven _____ his teeth. Then he _____ his face and _____ his hair. After that, he _____ down the stairs. He _____ to the kitchen. There, he _____ his breakfast. Later, he _____ for the bus at the corner.

At school, Steven _____ to the teacher. He _____ his books. At lunch, he _____ with his friends. After school, he _____ basketball with his team mates.

 C. Some verbs express action that you cannot see or hear. It might be a mental action.

Jennie **thought** about her problems.

Read the sentences. Write the verb from each sentence.
1. Tom missed his dog.
2. Bertha thought about her future.
3. Jerry dreams of his childhood.
4. We all wished for a sunny day.
5. Jessica imagined a better world.
6. The sick woman suffered with a fever.
7. Phil decided on a piece of peach pie.
8. The four friends planned a party.
9. We felt too hot in the noon sun.
10. Shelly forgot her new phone number.

D. Some sentences have more than one verb.

Mike **ran** and **jumped** all day.

Rewrite the sentences. Underline the two or more verbs in each sentence.
1. The sick child tossed and turned all night.
2. The letter blew out of my hand and flew away.
3. Liz put food on the plate and gave it to Al.
4. Patty weeded the garden, watered the lawn, and fixed the fence.
5. The plane flew over the airport before it landed.

Lesson 21 Linking Verbs

linking verb a word that tells what is or seems to be

A **linking verb** tells what is or seems to be. The most common linking verb is *be*. The forms of *be* are *am, is, are, was,* and *were.*

A. Sometimes a linking verb connects words that mean the same thing.

Don **is** my brother.

Tonight, our dessert **is** pie.

Spot **was** a big dog.

We **are** fast runners.

Read the sentences. In each sentence, find the form of the linking verb *be.* Write the words that mean the same thing. The first one is done for you.

1. We are all friends on this ski trip.
   we ⟶ friends
2. We were students at the same ski school.
3. I am the oldest person in the class.
4. Ellen was a ski instructor last year.
5. Maria is a terrific skier.
6. Barbara was the first person in the lift line.
7. My brothers were winners in the racing events.
8. The judges are cousins of mine.
9. Snowface is the name of the lodge.
10. The lodge was an old barn.

B. Sometimes a linking verb connects a word with a description.

Jason **is** strong.

The pie **was** sweet.

Rewrite the sentences. In each sentence, underline the form of the linking verb *be*. Draw an arrow to the word that describes another word. The first one is done for you.

1. The sky was blue.

   The sky <u>was</u> blue.
2. The dogs were frightened.
3. A rainy day is often cold.
4. The girls are comfortable here.
5. I am serious about this.
6. The clerk was too busy to wait on me.
7. The baseball fans were angry.
8. The tomatoes are almost ripe.
9. I am extremely lucky to know you!
10. Carlo is the best artist.

C. Some linking verbs express what *seems* to be. Ask yourself if the verb relates to your senses—sight, smell, touch, taste, or hearing. If so, it is probably a linking verb.

sense of sight ⟶ The sky **appears** gray.

sense of hearing ⟶ The music **sounds** too loud.

sense of touch ⟶ This kitten **feels** soft.

Rewrite the sentences. Underline the linking verb that relates to the senses.

1. Your plan sounds good to me.
2. The pumpkin pie smells delicious.
3. This soup tastes salty.
4. The floor feels sticky.
5. The firefighters look tired.
6. The dolphins sound happy.
7. Lydia looks pretty in blue.
8. The kitten seems healthy.
9. The milk smells sour.
10. Velvet feels soft.

Lesson 22   Present Tense Verbs

tense the verb form that shows the *time* of the verb's action or being—past, present, or future

present tense verb a word that expresses action or being in the present time (now)

A verb changes form to show *when* something happens. Is the action happening now? Did it happen in the past? Will it happen in the future? The time a verb shows is called its **tense.**

A. Is the action happening now? If it is in the present time, use a **present tense verb**.

> present tense verbs ⟶ run, sing, is, listens

Read each sentence. Rewrite each sentence and underline each present tense verb.

1. Beth picks apples from the tree.
2. Kate puts the clothes in the washer.
3. Jim folds the laundry for his family.
4. Ted climbs the ladder.
5. Ed walks down the trail.
6. Leah is happy.

B. The subject of a sentence can be singular or plural. Verbs with singular subjects do not end with *s*. However, verbs with singular subjects do end in *s* when the subject is *he, she, it,* a *person's name,* or an *object*.

> singular ⟶ I look at the rain.
>
> subjects ⟶ You run up the stairs.
>
> object ⟶ The **baby** laughs.
>
> person's name ⟶ **Ralph** kicks the ball.

Reminder

The subject of a sentence is the noun that performs the action.

Rewrite each sentence. Choose the correct form of the verb that completes each sentence.

1. I (cook, cooks) dinner.
2. You (like, likes) old movies.
3. The boy (play, plays) baseball.
4. José (plant, plants) tomatoes.
5. The dog (listen, listens) to Carmen.

Rewrite the sentences. Choose a verb from the box to complete each sentence. You will not use all the verbs.

walk/walks	shut/shuts	belong/belongs
draw/draws	save/saves	use/uses

6. He _____ the door behind him.
7. I _____ four cups of flour for this recipe.
8. She _____ pictures of outdoor scenes.
9. It _____ to the little girl over there.
10. Do you _____ ten dollars a week?
11. Ralph _____ two miles a day to stay healthy

C. Two or more nouns or pronouns are often used as a subject with one verb. Verbs with plural subjects do not end in s.

    plural subjects ⟶ **Max and Pat** eat lunch together.

                  We sing at church.

Reminder

The subject of a sentence is the noun that performs the action.

Rewrite each sentence. Choose the correct form of the verb that completes each sentence.

1. Tom and his brother (ride, rides) horses.
2. Tom and I (ride, rides) motorcycles.
3. Mary and her dad (feed, feeds) the livestock during the week.
4. We (feed, feeds) the livestock on weekends.
5. You and I (go, goes) to the same school.

Rewrite the sentences. Choose the verb from the box to complete each sentence.

listen	listens	like	likes

6. Tom and his sister _____ horses.
7. Both Lisa and her friend _____ horses.
8. Mary and I _____ to rock music.
9. Don and his brothers _____ only to rock music.
10. I _____ hamburgers and tacos.
11. Do you _____ to the radio in the morning?

Lesson 23   Regular Past Tense Verbs

Words to Know

past tense verb a word that expresses action or being that has already happened

regular past tense verb a word that forms the past tense by adding *-ed* or *-d*

vowels the letters *a, e, i, o, u,* and sometimes *y*

Reminder

Past, present, and *future* are three verb tenses. A verb's tense shows the time of its action or being.

A.   A **past tense verb** tells when an action has already happened. To form the past tense, most verbs add *-ed* or *-d* to the plural form of the present tense. These are called **regular past tense verbs.**

> present tense ⟶ They **visit** their aunt on Tuesdays.

> past tense ⟶ They **visited** Aunt Jane last Sunday, too.

To talk about past action, use a past tense verb.

Read each group of verbs. Choose and write the past tense verb from the group.

1. walks, walk, walked
2. turned, turns, turn
3. peel, peeled, peels
4. count, counts, counted
5. calls, called, call

B.   Some regular past tense verbs end in *-d*. Some end in *-ed*. How do you know which ending to use? If the present tense verb ends in *e*, just add *-d* to form the past tense. If the present tense verb does not end in *e*, add *-ed* to form the past tense.

> hire ⟶ hire**d**

> kick ⟶ kick**ed**

Write each verb in regular past tense form.

1. jump
2. believe
3. care
4. climb
5. fish
6. skate
7. save
8. seem
9. time
10. wait

C.   Some verbs form the regular past tense a little differently. Suppose a verb ends in a consonant with one **vowel** before it. Before adding -ed, you must double the consonant. This is true for words of one syllable.

clap —→ clap**ped**   stop —→ stop**ped**

A verb might end in a consonant with two vowels before it. For these words, you do not double the consonant before adding -ed.

pour —→ pour**ed**   soak —→ soak**ed**

Reminder

The consonants are all the other letters in the alphabet besides vowels.

Look at the verb in parentheses in each sentence. Copy the sentence with the correct past tense form of the verb.

1. After lunch, we (tip) the food server.
2. The lion (roar) loudly
3. The old man (stir) his coffee.
4. The lion (roam) from tree to tree.
5. Erica (star) in the school play.
6. The lights suddenly (dim).
7. The fruit slowly (rot) on the ground.
8. The boats (float) on the lake.

D.   To review, there are three ways to form the past tense of regular verbs. The first way is to add -ed. The second way is to add -d. The third way is to double the final consonant and add -ed.

work/work**ed**   slice/slice**d**   dip/dip**ped**

Read each sentence. Look at the verbs in parentheses. Rewrite the sentence with the correct form of the past tense verb.

1. The dog trainer (scold, scolded, scoldded) the poodle.
2. The dry cleaner (brush, brushed, brushhed) the wool coat.
3. Max (serve, serveed, served) the hungry men.
4. The family (plan, planed, planned) a party.

Lesson 24   Irregular Past Tense Verbs

Words to Know

irregular not usual

irregular past tense verb a word that does not form the past tense by adding *-ed* or *-d* to the present tense form

The word **irregular** means "not usual." The usual way to form the past tense is by changing the verb's ending. An **irregular past tense verb** does not change in this way. Some irregular past tense verbs change one or more letters in the middle.

run $\longrightarrow$ ran   swim $\longrightarrow$ swam

A. There are no rules to explain irregular verbs. You have to memorize these verb forms. Some verbs change a vowel to *a* to form the past tense.

give/gave	come/came	run/ran
begin/began	drink/drank	ring/rang
shrink/shrank	swim/swam	sing/sang

Copy each pair of sentences. Write the past tense of the verb to correctly complete the second sentence in each pair. Use verbs from the box above.

1. Joseph and Kim drink lots of water. Yesterday, they _____ eight glasses each.
2. Phil and his sisters swim on hot days. Last week, they _____ on Tuesday.
3. Classes begin on the hour. History class _____ 20 minutes ago.
4. The track team members run each afternoon. Yesterday, they _____ for more than an hour.
5. The students usually come home at four o'clock. Last year, they _____ home at three.
6. My cousins give me a birthday present every year. Last year, they _____ me a book.
7. The church bells usually ring at six o'clock. Yesterday, they _____ at five minutes after six.

Reminder

To *memorize* something is to study it until you remember it easily.

8. Some sweaters shrink in hot water. This blue one _____ in yesterday's wash.
9. Nat and Rachel sing together very well. They _____ for the first time a year ago.

B. Some verbs change *ow* to *ew* to form the past tense.

| know/knew | blow/blew | grow/grew | throw/threw |

Rewrite each pair of sentences with a verb pair from the box.

1. The Thompsons _____ out the garbage every evening. Yesterday, they _____ away two bags.
2. Tim and Jake always _____ what to do. When the dog ran away, they _____ where to find him.
3. Young children _____ very fast. Last year, Jasmine _____ four inches taller.
4. That desert wind can _____ very hard. Last night, it _____ down our tent.

C. To form the past tense, some verbs change one or more vowels to *o*.

speak ⟶ spoke

Rewrite each sentence with the correct past tense verb.

1. The water (freeze, froze) in the well last night.
2. We (spoke, speak) on the phone last week.
3. The bride's mother (wear, wore) a pink dress.
4. The thief (steal, stole) ten diamonds.
5. The father (drove, drive) his child to the doctor.
6. Lotta (tear, tore) the letter in half.

D. Some verbs change in other ways to form the past tense. Look at the examples in the box.

| do/did | bring/brought | see/saw | find/found |
| go/went | think/thought | take/took | speak/spoke |

Copy the story below. Choose the correct irregular past tense verb in each sentence.

Carla (go, went) to an interesting lecture last night. She (found, find) out some amazing facts about India. The speaker (speak, spoke) about a trip she (take, took) last year. She described many places she (went, go) during her travels. After the lecture, Carla (think, thought) she'd like to go to India, too.

Lesson 25 — To Be Verb Phrases

Words to Know

verb phrase a main verb and a helping verb that act as one verb

helping verb the part of a verb phrase that helps the main verb tell *what happens* or *is*

main verb the part of a verb phrase that tells about action or being

***to be* verb phrase** a verb phrase that uses *am, is, are, was,* or *were* as a helping verb

A **verb phrase** always has one or more helping verbs. A verb phrase also has a main verb. The **helping verb** helps the **main verb** tell what happens or is. Together these verbs tell about action or being. Look at the verb phrase below.

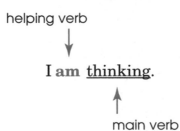

helping verb

I **am** <u>thinking</u>.

main verb

A. In a ***to be* verb phrase**, the helping verb is a form of the verb *to be*.

Rewrite each sentence. Underline the main verb in each sentence. Put a circle around the helping verb. The first one has been done for you.

1. The students are writing.
   The students (are) writing.
2. Jason is reading.
3. The cookies were baking.
4. I am making a plan.

B. Verb phrases with *am, is,* and *are* tell about action that is going on now. They are in the present tense. How can you decide which helping verb to use? Use *is* when the subject is singular. Use *am* when the subject is *I*. Use *are* when the subject is *plural*, and with *you*.

singular ⟶ A tree **is** growing outside my window.

plural ⟶ Weeds **are** growing in the garden.

Reminder

Past, present, and future **are** three verb tenses. A verb's tense shows the time of its action or being.

Look at the pictures. Read the partial sentences. Write a complete sentence using a *to be* verb phrase. Use *is* or *are* for the helping verb. For the main verb, use a word from the box. The first example is done for you.

Reminder

Singular means one. *Plural* means more than one.

| flying | playing | swimming | **singing** |

Sara is singing.

1. The bird

2. The boys

3. The musicians

C. Verb phrases with *was* and *were* tell about action that took place in the past. How can you tell which helping verb to use? Use *was* with singular subjects. Use *were* with plural subjects.

singular ⟶ Harry **was** hoping for a car.

plural ⟶ His parents **were** planning to surprise him.

Read the sentences and the words that follow. Rewrite each sentence with a *to be* verb phrase. Use *was* or *were* for the helping verb. The first example is done for you.

1. The children _____ the table. (setting)
   The children were setting the table.
2. The cat _____ on the chair. (sleeping)
3. Darlene _____ a letter. (writing)
4. The leaves _____ to the ground. (falling)
5. Sam _____ his bike. (riding)

Lesson 26 To Have Verb Phrases

to have verb a verb that is formed from the verb *to have*

to have verb phrase a verb phrase that uses *have, has,* or *had* as a helping verb

The forms of the **to have** verb are *have, has,* and *had.* Sometimes they are helping verbs. They are used with main verbs in a verb phrase.

helping verb

She (has) tried hard.

main verb

A. The main verb in a **to have** verb phrase often ends in *-d* or *-ed.*

We **have** danced a long time.

Sometimes the main verb ends in *-n* or *-en*.

I **have** eaten my dinner.

Copy each sentence. Underline the verb phrase in each sentence. Put a circle around the helping verb. The first one has been done for you.

1. The rock band had performed.
   The rock band (had) performed.
2. The dancer has practiced.
3. Selena has driven for years.
4. Jay had grown five tomatoes.
5. The ice cream had melted.
6. The boys had eaten the pie.
7. The sheep had jumped the fence.
8. We have visited Aunt Jane.
9. It has rained all night.
10. The boss has hired my sister.

B. Do you know when to use *have* and when to use *has* in a verb phrase? Follow these rules:

- With a singular subject, use **has** in a verb phrase.

  The <u>wolf</u> **has** howled for hours.

- With a plural subject, use **have** in a verb phrase.

  The <u>wolves</u> **have** howled for hours.

Reminder

Singular means "one." *Plural* means "more than one."

Copy each sentence. Choose *have* or *has* to correctly complete each sentence.

1. The workers _____ finished the bridge.
2. My dog _____ gained too much weight.
3. Our roses _____ bloomed.
4. Some stores _____ closed for the holiday.
5. A raindrop _____ fallen on my head.
6. The bakers _____ decorated all the cakes.
7. An eagle _____ landed on the mountain.
8. The goats _____ eaten the weeds.
9. The surfers _____ ridden great waves today.

C. In many sentences, pronouns tell who is acting. When a pronoun performs an action, follow these rules for writing *to have* verb phrases:

- Use the helping verb **have** when the pronoun is **I, you, we,** or **they.**

  I have traveled far and wide.

- Use the helping verb **has** when the pronoun is **he, she,** or **it.**

  He has moved from Texas.

Read the sentences. Choose *have* or *has* to complete each sentence.

1. It _____ been a month since you left.
2. I _____ always wanted a friend like you.
3. You _____ worked very hard this week.
4. She _____ wrapped the gifts in paper.
5. They _____ flown in small planes before.
6. He _____ earned a good living.
7. We _____ beaten all the odds.
8. It _____ been snowing all week.
9. They _____ sailed around the world.
10. He _____ cooked dinner.

Lesson 27 — To Do Verb Phrases

Words to Know

to do verb a verb that is formed from the verb **to do**

to do verb phrase a verb phrase that uses *do, did,* or *does* as a helping verb

Reminder

If you need to review main verbs and helping verbs, look back at Lesson 26.

Do, did, and *does* are forms of the **to do verb.** Sometimes they are helping verbs. They are used in verb phrases with main verbs.

A. The main verb in a **to do verb phrase** does not have an *s.* In this example, *know* is the main verb, *do* is the helping verb, and *do know* is the verb phrase.

> I **do know** what you mean.

Copy each sentence. Underline the verb phrase in each sentence. Put a circle around the helping verb.

1. The child does help.
2. My feet do hurt.
3. Carol did read that book.
4. The athlete did run fast.
5. Maria did wonder about that.

B. *Do* and *does* are used to tell about action in the present. *Did* is used to tell about action in the past.

Reminder

Write your sentences on a separate piece of paper.

Copy each sentence below. Choose the correct form of the helping verb that completes each sentence.

1. Yesterday, Don (do, did) throw away the trash.
2. Right now, Mary (does, did) understand the problem.
3. Today, the players (do, did) feel bad about losing.

C. *To do* verb phrases have three uses.

- To ask questions ⟶ **Does** anyone **care?**
- With the word *not* ⟶ I **do** not **care.**
- To make a strong point ⟶ The children **did enjoy** the park.

Look at the first of the three uses for a *to do* verb phrase on page 54. Notice that the words *does* and *care* are not together. The word *anyone* comes between them. But the helping verb and the main verb are still a verb phrase.

Read each sentence. Write the verb phrase in each. The first one is done for you.

1. Did you go to the ball park on opening day?
   did go
2. Sam did not talk to us.
3. Did Pat ride in our car?
4. The boys did not enjoy the game.
5. Does your mother know your friend?

D. Use *do* with plural subjects and *does* with singular subjects.

> **plural subject** ⟶ **Do bears** sleep all winter?
>
> **singular subject** ⟶ **Does** a **worm** feel pain?

Reminder
The subject of a sentence is the noun that performs the action.

Copy the sentences. Choose *do* or *does* to complete each sentence correctly.

1. Charlie _____ not like spinach.
2. The neighbors _____ have a nice garden.
3. Their son _____ water the lawn every day.
4. _____ the shoppers know about the sale?
5. _____ your family eat dinner at six?

E. Use *do* with the pronouns *I, you, we,* and *they.* Use *does* with the pronouns *he, she,* and *it.*

Do you like milk?

She does not eat sweets.

Look at the picture. Write a question the reporter might ask. Then write the answer that the winner might give. Use pronouns and *to do* verb phrases in your question and answer.

Lesson 28   Using Not with Verbs

not a word that denies something or says the opposite. *Not* gives an opposite meaning to a sentence.

adverb a part of speech that describes a verb

The word *not* is not part of a verb phrase. It usually comes *between* the words in a verb phrase.

A.   **Not** is a part of speech called an **adverb**. You will learn about adverbs in a later lesson. *Not* gives an opposite meaning to a sentence.

> **I do enjoy exercise** means the opposite of **I do not enjoy exercise.**

> **I do** understand. ⟶ **I do not** understand.

Read each sentence. Change the meaning of each sentence by adding *not*. Write a new sentence. The first one is done for you.

1. Sal is shopping today.

   Sal is not shopping today.

2. My best friend is moving to Oregon.
3. Dave was learning karate.
4. The teachers were taking a break.
5. The telephones are ringing.
6. Samantha has paid for her dance lessons.
7. The girls have worn sandals all summer.
8. Chuck had been on the phone for hours.
9. Diane does work at the market.
10. Marla did sign the card.

B. The word **not** changes the meaning of a question, too. Think about this: Sue and Jim went swimming today. Al and Kim will go swimming tomorrow. Look at the questions and answers below.

Who **has** gone swimming? ⟶ Sue, Jim

Who **has not** gone swimming? ⟶ Al, Kim

Read each question. Change each question by adding *not.* Write a new question.

1. Who had voted by five o'clock?
2. How many people are going to the pool?
3. Is Mary helping with the salad?
4. Was Mike enjoying the movie?
5. Did Kris get home on time?
6. Does Cathy care about her clothes?
7. Have you forgiven your sister?

C. A verb phrase includes only a main verb and a helping verb. Remember that the word *not* is not part of a verb phrase. Look at the example below.

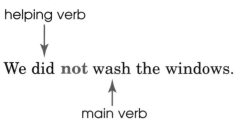

helping verb

We did **not** wash the windows.

main verb

Verb phrase ⟶ did wash

Read the sentences. Write the verb phrase in each sentence. The first one is done for you.

1. Sam Jones has not finished his paper.

   has finished

2. Aaron's clothes have not been washed.
3. Do you not understand the question?
4. I am not driving my car today.
5. Why have you not asked for help?
6. Marcy is not going with us.
7. That office is not hiring new clerks.
8. They are not enjoying their vacation.
9. Our flight did not leave right on time.
10. Have the workers finished, or not?

Lesson 29 Future Tense Verbs

Words to Know

future tense verb a verb that tells of action or being in the future

Reminder

Past, present, and *future* are three verb tenses. A verb's tense shows the time of its action or being.

A **future tense verb** tells of action or being in the future. To make the future tense, use the word *will* with the main verb. Together, the helping verb and the main verb are called a *verb phrase.*

> We will march together. They will watch us.

A. The future tense is always made up of more than one word. The helping verb is *will.* The main verb does not have an *s.*

helping verb

We will eat at five o'clock.

main verb

You will finish your homework.

future tense verb phrase

Copy the sentences. Underline the future tense verb phrase. Put a circle around the helping verb. The first one is done for you.

1. The jazz band will perform later.
   The jazz band will perform later.
2. I will listen carefully.
3. The crowd will enjoy the music.
4. Tony will play the banjo.
5. We will serve a picnic lunch.
6. The sandwiches will be tasty.

7. Everyone will eat watermelon.
8. Shawn will watch the baby.
9. She will talk to her mother.
10. Sparky will bark.

B. In the future tense, the main verb does not have an *s*. You just write the helping verb.

      verb with singular subject ⟶ **He sings.**

      verb with plural subject ⟶ **They sing.**

      future verbs ⟶ I **will sing.** They **will sing.** He **will sing.**

Read the sentences. Notice that the verbs are in the present tense. Change the sentence to put the verb in the future tense. Write a new sentence. The first one is done for you.

1. I take a class on Wednesday nights.

   I will take a class on Wednesday nights.

2. Jason and Margo write letters to each other.
3. We need a new roof.
4. Gina and Blake visit their grandma in the spring.
5. They buy their school supplies in August.
6. I wear size 10 in running shorts.
7. The horses run very fast in the race.
8. You need to wear a hat tomorrow.
9. Shani takes a piano lesson tomorrow.
10. Nick walks the dog after school.

Read the story below. Notice that the underlined verbs are all in the present tense. Rewrite the story and change all of the underlined verbs to the future tense.

11. Matt and Lana are making plans for spring vacation. They <u>go</u> to the city to visit their grandparents. There they <u>attend</u> a concert. They also <u>see</u> a new display at the science museum.
When they get home, Matt <u>cleans</u> the garage, and Lana <u>sorts</u> through their books and clothes. They <u>send</u> what they don't use to cousins in South America. The vacation week <u>goes</u> quickly. But Matt and Lana <u>have</u> fun.

Lesson 30 Other Helping Verbs

helping verb the part of a verb phrase that helps the main verb tell about what happens or is

A **helping verb** is always used with a main verb.

helping verb

You **should get** to class on time.

main verb

Reminder

In a verb phrase, the main verb tells what happens or what is.

A. The words *can, could, may, might, must, should,* and *would* are helping verbs. To make verb phrases, they are used with main verbs.

I **can run** 3 miles.

They **might go** to the party.

You **should call** before 4:00.

Copy each sentence. Underline the verb phrase. Circle the helping verb. The first one is done for you.

1. I would like some dessert.
   I (would) like some dessert.
2. My brother can hit home runs.
3. You must pay this bill soon.
4. We can watch TV until 10:00.
5. We could go away on vacation.
6. Joe might visit in April.
7. You may open the gift now.
8. Steve should get a haircut.

B. Using a helping verb changes the main verb. The main verb in a verb phrase does not have an *s* on the end.

She **eats** an apple every day.

She **should eat** an apple every day.

Choose the main verb that correctly completes each sentence.
Copy the corrected sentences.

1. The boys should (help, helps) their friend.
2. They might (travel, travels) to Greece this summer.
3. I must (find, finds) my lost dog!
4. Henry might (give, gives) Vincent a loan.
5. Yolanda can (help, helps) herself to an ice cream.
6. He could (walk, walks) across the bridge each way.
7. The cat may (remain, remains) inside tonight.
8. Your aunt would (like, likes) to see you.

C.

Different helping verbs have different meanings. Think about the meaning of *can, must,* and *should.* Each word changes the meaning of the verb phrase. Can means "able to". Must means "required to". Should means "ought to".

For example, the fact that you *can* do something does not mean that you *should* do it.

Use phrases from the box to complete the sentences. (You will not use all the words in the box.) Circle the helping verb and underline the main verb.

Reminder

Write your sentences on a separate piece of paper.

sing songs	eat the right foods	study more
save money	breathe clean air	walk to school
drink more water	floss my teeth	jump high
dance well	take out the trash	wash the dishes
get more exercise	write a letter	run fast

Things I **Can** Do
1. I can _____.   2. I can _____.
3. I can _____.   4. I can _____.

Things I **Must** Do
5. I must _____.   6. I must _____.
7. I must _____.   8. I must _____.

Things I **Should** Do
9. I should _____.   10. I should _____.
11. I should _____.   12. I should _____.

Lesson 31 Direct and Indirect Objects

Words to Know

direct object the noun or pronoun that *receives* the action of a verb

indirect object the noun or pronoun *to whom* or *for whom* an action is done

A **direct object** tells what receives the action of the verb. Direct objects are important in speaking and writing. Without them, you could hardly describe a dinner. You couldn't say you set the *table*. You couldn't say you held a *fork*. You couldn't say you ate the *food*.

A. Direct objects follow action verbs. They never follow linking verbs. But not every action verb has a direct object.

Reminder

Many linking verbs are forms of the verb *to be:* am, is, are, was, were.

sentence with a
direct object ⟶ The choir members sang a **song.**

sentence without a
direct object ⟶ The choir members sang beautifully.

After an action verb, direct objects answer the question *What?* or *Whom?*

Gina answered the **phone.**
↑
what

Marc welcomed the **visitor.**
↑
whom

Read each sentence. Write the word that is a direct object.
Remember: Direct objects answer the question *What?* or *Whom?*

1. The fielder caught the ball.
2. The batter dropped her bat.
3. My sister sailed the boat.
4. He enjoys math problems.
5. Tammy bought a used motorcycle.
6. Bill wants new skates.
7. Tammy and Bill drank milk.
8. The surfer rode the giant waves.

B.   An **indirect object** tells *to whom* or *for whom* an action was done. It comes right after the verb and before the direct object. Hint: Indirect objects do not follow the words *to* or *for*. But the word *to* or *for* is understood.

>   Phil gave **Stella** some photos.

>   Lew read **us** his new poem.

Read each sentence. Write the indirect object. Use the question in parentheses to help. The first one is done for you.

1. Throw Sandy a towel, please. (Who will catch the towel?)
   Sandy
2. Josh sent Linda a birthday card. (Who will get the card?)
3. Phong asked the teacher a question. (Who did he ask?)
4. Alex read his little brother a story. (Whom did Alex read to?)
5. Marty bought his sister a straw hat. (Who will get the hat?)
6. She told us the story of her life. (Whom did she tell the story to?)
7. Hank bought himself a present. (Whom was the present for?)
8. Tony gave Sharon a phone call. (Who did Tony call?)

C.   Direct objects and indirect objects are always nouns or pronouns. When they are pronouns, they must be in objective pronoun form.

>   direct object ⟶ Cathy met **him** last week.

>   indirect object ⟶ Jake gave **us** some flowers.

Reminder

If you need to review the objective form of pronouns, look back at Lesson 15.

Read each sentence and the pronouns in parentheses. Choose the pronoun that completes the sentence correctly. Rewrite the completed sentences.

1. I showed (he, him) my best design.
2. Ms. Fox gave (we, us) a B on the project.
3. Please tell (I, me) everything he said!
4. The clerk sold (she, her) a matching belt.
5. We sent (they, them) a nice wedding present.

Lesson 32	What Is an Adjective?

Words to Know

adjective the part of speech that describes a noun or pronoun

article the most common adjectives are the articles *a, an,* and *the*

The word *adjective* sounds like AJ-ihk-tiv.

A word that describes a noun or pronoun is an **adjective**. Most adjectives tell *what kind, which one,* or *how many.*

A.   Think about words like *red* and *round*. These words could help you describe an apple.

Read each word listed below. Write the words that could describe a noun or pronoun. You should be able to find 18 adjectives.

of	blue	thin	into	for
but	how	funny	bright	wow
small	are	herself	heavy	hard
nice	if	however	sick	into
why	wild	under	windy	yellow
and	black	sunny	or	along
nor	loud	be	am	wide
strong	yours	also	beside	tall

B.   In different sentences, the same word can be a different part of speech. How can you tell what part of speech it is? Look at what the word *does*. If it describes a noun or a pronoun, it is an adjective.

adjective   noun   adjective   noun

I ate the **red** apple.   I did not eat the **apple** core.

Write each pair of words listed below. Circle the adjective in each pair.

1. tiny leaf
2. leafy vegetables
3. vegetable soup
4. soup bowl
5. student desk
6. new student
7. writing paper
8. paper doll
9. red tomato
10. tomato soup

C. Here's a hint about finding adjectives. Look for the noun or pronoun first. Then ask the questions. *What kind? Which one?* and *How many?* An adjective will tell the answer.

They put up a **picket** fence.

Picket answers the question *What kind of fence?*

I want **that** pair of shoes.

That answers the question *Which pair of shoes?*

Four boys joined the team.

Four answers the question *How many boys?*

Write the noun in each sentence. Write and circle the adjective that describes it. Then, write the question the adjective answers. Choose from the questions in the box.

What kind?	Which one?	How many?

1. You need red shoes.
2. He ate two sandwiches.
3. She already saw that movie.
4. We wrote many postcards.
5. The package arrived three hours ago.
6. I bought chocolate cookies.

D. The words *a, an,* and *the* are a special kind of adjective. They are called **articles**. An article always comes before a noun. Another adjective might also come before the noun.

    a tree   **a tall** tree

Copy the sentences. Circle all of the articles.
1. The big dog jumped over the fence.
2. Sara peeled an orange and threw away the peel.
3. Pat wrote a letter to the company.

E. Use *a* before words that begin with a consonant. Use *an* before words that begin with a vowel.

    a train   **an** automobile

Reminder

Vowels are *a, e, i, o, u,* and sometimes *y*. Consonants are all other letters.

Write each sentence. Choose *a* or *an* to complete each sentence.
1. Joe bought _____ bag of apples.
2. Meg baked _____ apple pie.
3. Flo ran _____ good race.
4. The judges gave the winner _____ medal.

Lesson 33 Adjectives After Linking Verbs

Words to Know **linking verb** a word that tells what is or seems to be

Reminder

You have learned that some linking verbs are *am, is, was, are,* and *were.*

Adjectives do not always come before the word they describe. Sometimes they come *after* the word. When they do, they are joined to the word by a **linking verb.**

A. The same adjective might be used *after* a linking verb or *before* a noun.

the **blue** box   The box is **blue.**

When the adjective comes after a linking verb, it describes the noun before the linking verb.

The **peppers** are too **hot.**

Copy each sentence. Draw an arrow from the adjective that comes after the linking verb to the noun that the adjective describes.

1. This car is new.
2. My sister is strong.
3. The dream was scary.
4. Mel's cat appears ill.
5. The flowers smell sweet.

B. More than one adjective can come after a linking verb. All the adjectives are describing the same noun.

The **dog** was **cold** and **hungry.**

Copy each sentence. Circle all the adjectives that are not articles. Underline the word that the adjectives describe. The first one is done for you.

1. Lou is sick and tired of this.
   Lou is (sick) and (tired) of this.
2. Margo seems ready, willing, and able to sing.
3. Tim appears healthy and happy today.
4. Does Ellen feel excited or disappointed?
5. The vegetables were washed, sliced, and cooked.

6. The music was boring, flat, and off-key.
7. The weather was warm and pleasant.
8. The day was sunny, calm, and clear.
9. Ben sounded frantic and frightened on the phone.

C.

Adjectives that describe pronouns usually come *after* linking verbs.

You look **marvelous**.

Choose an adjective from the box that completes each sentence. Write each completed sentence.

angry	fresh	beautiful
quiet	taller	funny

1. After the baby's bath, she felt _____ and clean.
2. Everyone laughed at the joke because it was so _____ .
3. I thought she was more _____ than the other model.
4. With that frown on his face, he looks _____ .
5. Since last year, they have all grown _____ .
6. Everyone else talked, but she remained _____ .

D.

Adjectives that describe nouns can come before the noun or after a linking verb.

There's the **old** barn.   The barn is **old**.

Read each pair of words. Write a short sentence in which the words appear together. The first one is done for you.
1. black cat
   There's the black cat.
2. wooden bat
3. red rose
4. grilled hamburger
5. seven shoes
6. big sailboat

Read each pair of words. Write a short sentence. Place a linking verb between the adjective and the noun. The first one is done for you.
7. ugly toad
   The toad is ugly.
8. loud music
9. blue sky
10. happy sisters
11. hot pizza
12. fast jog

Lesson 34 Proper Adjectives

Words to Know   **proper adjective** an adjective formed from a proper noun

All adjectives tell about people, places, and things. All adjectives describe nouns and pronouns.

adjectives⟶ **ancient** mummy
new camera
blond child

A **proper adjective** does that, too. But there is a difference. Proper adjectives are made from proper nouns. They describe by *name*. They are always capitalized, just like proper names.

proper adjectives⟶ **Egyptian** mummy
German camera
Swedish child

A. Names can be used both as nouns and adjectives. Sometimes a name stays just as it is when it is used to describe.

Reminder

A proper noun names a particular person, place, thing, event, or idea.

proper noun ⟶ **Jack London** wrote adventure stories.

proper adjective ⟶ She likes **Jack London** stories.

Copy each sentence. Underline the proper adjective or adjectives for each.
1. The Mojave is a California desert.
2. Dr. Smith enjoys Stephen King books.
3. Major Jones wears a U.S. Army uniform.
4. Samuel Morse invented the Morse code.
5. Crunchies cereal is Mara's favorite kind.
6. Jeff wants a French poodle.
7. Lisa is interested in Russian history.
8. Lake Shore Drive is a Chicago landmark.

B. Many proper adjectives are *forms* of proper nouns. The name is not used just as it is. The end of the name changes.

> **proper nouns**⟶ America, China, Egypt
>
> **proper adjectives**⟶ American, Chinese, Egyptian

Read the proper nouns in List 1. Choose a proper adjective from List 2 that best matches. Write both together.

List 1	**List 2**
1. France	a. Cuban
2. Greece	b. Spanish
3. Scotland	c. Greek
4. Spain	d. French
5. Cuba	e. Scottish
6. Japan	f. Japanese

C. Proper adjectives and proper nouns may look just the same. They both begin with a capital letter. How do you tell the difference? Proper adjectives always describe something else. Proper nouns don't.

Look for the noun or pronoun being described. Rewrite the sentences. Be sure to capitalize the proper adjectives.

1. The florida team beat the arizona team.
2. High winds hit the pacific coastline.
3. Her dress is made of fine french lace.
4. april showers bring may flowers.
5. She thinks greek olives are too salty.

D. In a sentence, a proper adjective describes the noun or nouns that come after it.

proper adjective   noun

Uncle Mike is an **Irish citizen.**

Copy each sentence. Circle the proper adjective. Then underline the noun it describes. The first one is done for you.

1. The Changs own three ⟨Chinese⟩ restaurants.
2. Caesar was a great Roman emperor.
3. Ruben has a large Mexican blanket.
4. Pizza is Herman's favorite Italian food.

Lesson 35   Comparative Adjectives

Words to Know   **comparative adjective** an adjective used to compare two or more nouns or pronouns

Almost any adjective can be made into a **comparative adjective.** Usually, the ending is changed.

adjectives ⟶ small, high

comparative adjectives ⟶ smaller, highest

A. To compare two people, places, or things, add *-er* to the adjective. To compare three or more, add *-est* to the adjective.

Jerry is **shorter** than Al.

The **tallest** girl in the class is Cindy.

Read each sentence and the adjectives in parentheses. Choose the correct form of the adjective that completes each sentence. Write each complete sentence.

1. Sally's jacket is (newer, newest) than Patty's.
2. This hamster has the (thicker, thickest) coat of all the hamsters here.
3. Dave's room is (clean, cleaner) than Michael's room.
4. That is the (deeper, deepest) hole our dog has ever dug.
5. The (faster, fastest) runner of all won the race.
6. Which animal is (smarter, smartest), a dog or a pig?
7. The (younger, youngest) of the four sisters is named Ellie.
8. This movie is (longer, longest) than that one.
9. My cat is (friskier, friskiest) than Darlene's cat.
10. This is the (wetter, wettest) spring I can remember.

B. Sometimes, the spelling of the adjective changes when an ending is added. Study the rules.

- Sometimes an adjective ends with a consonant that has one vowel before it. In this case, double the consonant. Then add *-er* or *-est*.

  hot ⟶ ho**tt**er ⟶ ho**tt**est

  fat ⟶ fa**tt**er ⟶ fa**tt**est

- Sometimes an adjective ends with a *y* that has a consonant before it. In this case, change the *y* to *i*. Then add *-er* or *-est*.

  heavy ⟶ heav**i**er ⟶ heav**i**est

  dry ⟶ dr**i**er ⟶ dr**i**est

Read each adjective. Write the form that compares two people or things. Then write the form that compares three or more.

1. big
2. hungry
3. tasty
4. wet
5. shiny
6. flat
7. fit
8. sad

C. If an adjective ends in *e*, just add *-r* or *-st* to make it a comparative.

  brave ⟶ brave**r** ⟶ brave**st**

Read each sentence and the adjective in parentheses. How many people or things are being compared? Write each sentence with the correct form of the adjective.

1. Which is (safe), flying or driving?
2. The (large) of the five men came forward.
3. This rope is (loose) than that one.
4. The (little) of the six kittens was the one I wanted.
5. Tune in for the (late) news.
6. The (fine) lace in the whole store was used.
7. This is the (blue) sky I have ever seen.
8. My teacher is (nice) than yours.
9. The big truck is (wide) than the little truck.

Lesson 36 Irregular Comparative Adjectives

Words to Know

irregular comparative adjective an adjective that does not form the comparative by adding *-er* or *-est*

Many adjectives form the comparative by adding *-er* or *-est*. An **irregular comparative adjective** does not. You must use the words *more, most, less,* or *least* with some of these adjectives. Other irregular adjectives change their form entirely.

Reminder

A *syllable* is a part of a word with a sound of its own. The word *baseball* has two syllables: *base•ball.* The word beautiful has three: *beau•ti•ful.*

A. Some adjectives have three or more syllables. Some adjectives end in *-ful.* With these adjectives, use *more* or *most* to make comparisons. Use *more* when comparing two people or things. Use *most* when comparing three or more.

talented ⟶ **more** talented ⟶ **most** talented

The singer was **more talented** than the juggler.

helpful ⟶ **more** helpful ⟶ **most** helpful

Out of all the salesmen, he was **most helpful**.

Read each sentence and the adjective in parentheses. Write the correct form of the adjective that completes the sentence. Use *more* or *most.*

1. The (entertaining) party we went to all year was Susan's.
2. Of all the workers in the shop, Paul is the (skillful)
3. Do you think Austin is (interesting) than San Antonio?
4. The (useful) tool in the toolbox is this hammer.
5. Claire has a (dramatic) style than Chris.

B. Use *less* when comparing two people or things. Use *least* when comparing three or more. Follow this rule even for adjectives of one syllable.

full ⟶ less full ⟶ least full

difficult ⟶ less difficult ⟶ least difficult

Read each sentence and the adjective in parentheses. Write each sentence with the correct form of the adjective. Use *less* or *least*.

1. Brad's dog is (happy) than Tony's.
2. The big store has the (expensive) books of all.
3. That dry log is (slippery) than this wet one.
4. This meat is (tender) than it was yesterday.
5. This is the (attractive) of the four offers.

C. The forms of the adjective *good* are *good, better,* and *best.* Use *better* to compare two people or things. Use *best* to compare three or more.

This pencil writes **better** than that one.

This is the **best** pencil of all for drawing.

Write complete sentences. Write *good, better,* or *best* to fill each blank.

1. Alfie is a _____ dog.
2. Alfie is a _____ dog than Freckles.
3. Fearless is the _____ dog of all.
4. We are looking for a _____ deal on a car.
5. This ad says they have the _____ deals in town.
6. My brother can give me a _____ deal than that.
7. Joan's haircut looks _____ than Lana's.
8. Lana got a _____ haircut at the beauty salon.
9. Cindy's haircut is the _____ one I've seen.

D. The forms of the adjective *bad* are *bad, worse,* and *worst.* Use *worse* to compare two people or things. Use *worst* to compare three or more.

Write complete sentences. Write *bad, worse,* or *worst* to fill each blank.

1. Sammy's dog did a _____ thing today.
2. What Jim's dog did was even _____.
3. The _____ of all was what Stan's dog did.
4. Have you ever had a _____ day?
5. The _____ day I ever had was yesterday.
6. It was even _____ than last Saturday.
7. The _____ movie I ever saw is now in video.
8. Did you ever see anything _____ than this?
9. If you think that's _____, look at this one!

Lesson 37 What Is an Adverb?

adverb the part of speech that tells more about a verb, adjective, or other adverb

Adverbs are very useful. They help you describe actions. Adverbs usually tell four things: *when, where, how,* or *how often.*

A. Suppose you want to tell *how* you did something. To describe an action, you would use an adverb. Someone who speaks *softly* sounds different from someone who speaks *loudly.* Without adverbs, you couldn't describe the difference.

Not all adverbs end in *-ly.* But if a word ends in *-ly,* there's a good chance it's an adverb.

Read the words listed below. Write the adverbs. You should be able to find 10 of them.

the	house	carefully	herself
his	rapidly	look	seriously
coldly	really	is	hello
lately	home	ice	honestly
lie	light	leg	happily
directly	tenderly	kitchen	little
leaves	joke	camp	park

B. Adverbs do more than just tell *how.* Some adverbs tell *where.*

where ⟶ outside, anywhere

Copy the sentences. Underline the adverb that tells *where.*
1. Put that book here.
2. Wanda played inside on the rainy day.
3. Each person took one step backward.
4. We put the lemon tree outdoors.
5. We kept the fern indoors.
6. I looked everywhere for my lost watch.

C. Adverbs do more than just tell *how* or *where*. Some adverbs tell *when* something was done.

when ———▶ then, now, early

Read the sentences and adverbs in parentheses. Rewrite each sentence with the adverb that tells *when*.

1. I need to see you (soon, clearly).
2. The letter should arrive (somewhere, tomorrow).
3. (Yesterday, Kindly), we had a picnic lunch.
4. Was it (here, today) that we planned to meet?
5. Go to the principal's office (now, upstairs).
6. (Indoors, Later), we will review your homework.

D. Adverbs do more than just tell *how, where,* or *when.* Some adverbs tell *how many times* something was done.

how many times ———▶ once, never, often

Copy each sentence. Circle the adverb that *tells how many times.*

1. Brian often visits this park.
2. Twice, he saw three deer by the pond.
3. Deer seldom come that close to people.

E. Adverbs make your writing more interesting. They help the reader imagine the actions you describe.

Look at the picture. Read the sentences that tell about it. Make each sentence more interesting by adding an adverb.

early	slowly	loudly	often
late	outside	together	inside

1. They arrived at the dance.
2. The band played.
3. They danced.
4. They left.

Lesson 38 Adjective Modifiers

adjective modifier an adverb that describes an adjective

Adverbs do more than describe verbs. They can also describe adjectives.

verb adverb

describes a *verb* ⟶ She laughed **loudly**.

adverb adjective

describes an *adjective* ⟶ She had a **very** loud laugh.

The word *modifier* sounds like MAW-dih-feye-uhr.

A. An adverb can give more information about an adjective. It might tell *how much, how little,* or *to what degree.* An adverb that describes an adjective is an **adjective modifier.**

Write the word pairs. Underline the adjective and circle the adjective modifier, or adverb. The first one is done for you.

1. quite famous
   (quite) famous
2. entirely possible
3. nearly finished
4. almost late
5. hardly visible
6. terribly hungry
7. fairly happy
8. completely full
9. absolutely delighted
10. sincerely sorry

B. How can you find adverbs that tell more about adjectives? Look for the adjective first. Then ask these questions: *How much? How little? To what degree?* An adverb will tell the answer.

That pie made me **completely** full.

Completely answers the question *How much?*

Frances was **hardly** aware of the danger.

Hardly answers the question *How little?*

Stan was **particularly** helpful.

Particularly answers the question *To what degree?*

Copy each sentence. Then underline the adjective. Next, circle the adverb that tells more about it. The first one is done for you.

1. Diane was extremely bored.
   Diane was (extremely) bored.
2. The movie was overly violent.
3. The popcorn was too salty.
4. The day was almost ruined.
5. We were nearly soaked in the rain.
6. That was a truly scary story.
7. The rainbow is exceptionally clear.
8. The weather is getting somewhat colder.
9. This food is barely warm.
10. The guests are rather amusing.

C. Using adverbs as adjective modifiers can make your writing more interesting. Adverbs can help the reader imagine the scene you are describing.

Read the sentences that tell about the picture. Add adverbs to tell more about the underlined adjectives. Tell *how much, how little,* or *to what degree.*

very	quite	completely	absolutely
too	truly	incredibly	so

1. The waterfall was <u>beautiful</u>.
2. The deer's antlers were <u>big</u>.
3. The frog's croaking was <u>loud</u>.
4. The <u>tall</u> tree whispered in the wind.

Lesson 39   Adverb Modifiers

adverb modifier an adverb that describes or limits another adverb

You already know that adverbs describe verbs and adjectives. They can also describe other adverbs.

                                               verb   adverb
                                                ↓   ↓
describes a *verb* ⟶ He waited **patiently**.

                                               adverb   adjective
                                                ↓   ↓
describes an *adjective* ⟶ He's a **very** patient person.

                                               adverb   adverb
                                                ↓   ↓
describes an *adverb* ⟶ He waited **very** patiently.

A. An adverb that describes another adverb is called an **adverb modifier**. It might tell *how much, how little,* or *to what degree.*

Read each sentence. The underlined word in each sentence is an adverb that describes another adverb. Write the word that the underlined adverb describes. The first one is done for you.

1. I ran <u>very</u> fast.
    fast
2. You dance <u>quite</u> well.
3. He drops the ball <u>too</u> often.
4. She sings <u>rather</u> poorly.
5. I woke up <u>really</u> early.
6. He spends money <u>somewhat</u> foolishly.
7. Ed works <u>unusually</u> hard.
8. We hiked <u>quite</u> far from camp.
9. She listened <u>especially</u> carefully.
10. Bob acted <u>truly</u> unselfishly.

B. Here's a hint about finding adverb modifiers. First look for the adverb that tells more about the verb. Then ask the questions *How much? How little?* and *To what degree?* An adverb modifier will tell the answer.

The kitten was treated **very** gently.
The word *very* answers the question *How much?*

Gene was **barely** there for a minute.
The word *barely* answers the question *How little?*

Tiffany spoke **rather** unkindly about Kim.
The word *rather* answers the question *To what degree?*

Read the sentence pairs. Notice that the same word is underlined in both sentences. Rewrite the sentence that uses the word as an *adverb modifier*.

1. a. I would <u>rather</u> read than watch TV.
   b. He answered each question <u>rather</u> carefully.
2. a. We go to track meets <u>fairly</u> often.
   b. Jonas didn't win the prize <u>fairly</u>.
3. a. I listened to him <u>quite</u> closely.
   b. She couldn't <u>quite</u> believe Ann's story.
4. a. Mary and Victor are <u>very</u> busy.
   b. They <u>very</u> rarely take a vacation.

Reminder

An adverb modifier describes another adverb.

C. Adverbs that tell more about other adverbs make your writing more interesting. They help the reader imagine what you are describing.

Read the sentences that tell about the picture. Notice the underlined adverbs. Now add an adverb to the space in each sentence. Rewrite the completed sentence. The word you add will tell *how much, how little,* or *to what degree*.

1. James throws the javelin _____ <u>forcefully</u>.
2. Darlene runs _____ <u>quickly</u>.
3. Jerome jumps _____ <u>easily</u>.

Lesson 40

When to Use an Adverb or an Adjective

Word to Know

modify tell more about a word; expand or limit its meaning

Adjectives and adverbs are a lot alike. Both are parts of speech that **modify**, or tell more about, other words.

A. How can you tell an adjective from an adverb? Two rules can help you decide which one to use. Always use adjectives to modify nouns and pronouns. Always use adverbs to modify verbs, adjectives, and other adverbs.

The child has **red** hair.

The adjective *red* modifies the noun *hair*.

The child plays **happily**

The adverb *happily* modifies the verb *plays*.

Use words from the box to complete each sentence. Write each completed sentence.

modify	adjectives	adverbs	speech

1. Both adjectives and adverbs are parts of _____ .
2. Adjectives _____ nouns and pronouns.
3. Adverbs modify verbs, _____ , and other _____.

B. Should you use an adjective or an adverb? If you are not sure, look at the word you want to modify. Is it a noun or a pronoun? If so, use an adjective. Is it a verb, an adjective, or another adverb? If so, use an adverb.

Read each sentence. Copy each underlined word. Write what part of speech it is. Write if you would use an adjective or an adverb to modify that part of speech. The first one is done for you.

1. Look at the <u>bridge</u>.
   bridge, noun, adjective
2. We <u>ran</u> across the street.
3. Here is a glass of <u>juice</u>.
4. Please <u>pass</u> the salt.
5. The boys <u>studied</u> all day.

Reminder

Adjectives answer these questions: *What kind? Which one? How many?* Adverbs answer these questions: *How? Where? When? How many times?*

6. Do you like my <u>dress</u>?
7. Our family got a <u>puppy</u>.
8. My <u>friends</u> met downtown.
9. Paul <u>raked</u> the leaves.

C. You can change many adjectives into adverbs. Usually, you just add *-ly*. Sometimes you must change a *y* to an *i* before adding *-ly*.

adjectives⟶ soft, quick, icy

adverbs⟶ soft**ly**, quick**ly**, ic**ily**

Read each sentence and the words in parentheses. Choose the adjective or adverb to complete the sentence. Rewrite each sentence.

1. We stood before the (open, openly) door.
2. The door opened (sudden, suddenly).
3. Jack read the story (eager, eagerly).
4. Pam has always been an (eager, eagerly) reader.
5. The cook worked (busy, busily) in the kitchen.
6. The cook was very (busy, busily).
7. The library is a place for (quiet, quietly) study.
8. They talked as (quiet, quietly) as possible in the library.

D. The word *good* is an adjective. Use it to modify nouns and pronouns. The word *well* is an adverb. Use it to modify verbs.

Michael is **good** at basketball.

The word *good* is an adjective after a linking verb. It modifies the noun *Michael*. It answers the question *What kind?*

Michael plays basketball **well**.

The word *well* is an adverb. It modifies the verb *plays*. It answers the question *How?*

Use *good* or *well* to complete each sentence. First, find the noun, pronoun, or verb that will be modified. If you find a noun or a pronoun, you should use *good*. If you find a verb, you should use *well*.

1. James is a very _____ dancer.
2. Carmen rides a horse quite _____.
3. These strawberries are very _____.
4. My mother is always _____ to me.
5. The bean plants are growing very _____.
6. Never wear a _____ shirt to paint the house.

Lesson 41　Avoiding Double Negatives

Words to Know
negative　one or more words that mean *no* or deny something

double negative　the mistaken use of two negatives instead of one to tell one negative idea

contraction　the shortened form of two words in which an apostrophe (') takes the place of the missing letter or letters

A **negative** is a word that says *no* or *not* to something. It is a mistake to use two negatives to tell one negative idea. This is called a **double negative.** The second negative says *no* to the first negative. It wipes out the meaning of what you meant to say. A double negative does not make sense and should be avoided.

correct use ——► Bev said nothing.

incorrect use ——► Bev did **not** say **nothing.**

A.　Many negatives have the word *no* in them: *no, not, no one, nobody, nothing, nowhere,* and *none.* Other negatives are *never, hardly, barely,* and *scarcely.*

Read each sentence. Find the negatives. Copy only the sentences that are correct. Hint: If there are two or more negatives, it is incorrect.

1. We have no bananas today.
2. The store did not have no bananas.
3. I do not understand the question.
4. I do not understand nothing you say.
5. Bert did not hardly even try.
6. Bert hardly tried.

B.　A **contraction** is a shortened form of two words. A negative is often part of a contraction. To make a contraction, an apostrophe takes the place of the missing letter or letters.

are not ——► aren't

Here are some other contractions and their meanings.

won't / will not   wouldn't / would not

didn't / did not   isn't / is not

haven't / have not   hasn't / has not

Read each sentence. Find the contraction. Rewrite the sentences using the two words the contraction stands for.

1. I wouldn't take that risk.
2. Lisa isn't a very good dancer.
3. Dustin hasn't had much practice.
4. The band members haven't arrived yet.
5. I didn't know you could dance.
6. Stan won't dance to fast songs.

C. Writing contractions is not hard. Look at the examples in exercise B. Just think about the meaning of each sentence. Combine the two words that mean what you want to say. Don't forget to use an apostrophe.

Look at the underlined words in each sentence. Rewrite the sentences using the correct contractions.

1. Our teacher will not be here tomorrow.
2. She was not feeling very well today.
3. We have not done our homework yet.
4. Our papers are not due until Monday.

D. All contractions are not negatives. Here are some contractions that are not negatives.

should've / should have   I'll / I will

you'll / you will   he's / he is

we'll / we will   she'd / she would

Read each sentence. Find the contraction and any negatives. All the sentences have two negatives. Rewrite each sentence correctly. Use only one negative in your new sentences.

1. Tommy wouldn't have said nothing about it.
2. We won't hardly notice the difference.
3. Those boys aren't going nowhere tonight.
4. She's scarcely done nothing all day.

Lesson 42 | Conjunctions and Sentence Parts

Words to Know

conjunction the part of speech used to join words, groups of words, and sentences

compound subject two or more connected subjects that have the same verb

compound predicate two or more connected verbs that have the same subject

Reminder

The subject of a sentence is the person or thing doing the action. The predicate is the words that follow the subject.

The subject of a sentence can have two or more parts. Sometimes the predicate of a sentence has two or more parts. When this happens, use a **conjunction,** a word used to join the parts. The word *and* is a conjunction.

subject ⟶ **Kurt** and **Cindy** played tennis.

predicate ⟶ Freddie **caught** the ball and **threw** the runner out.

A. Sometimes a conjunction joins single words. Sometimes a conjunction joins groups of words. The words in the box are conjunctions.

and	or	but	nor	for	so	yet

Will the boat sink **or** float?

Copy each sentence. Circle the conjunction in each sentence.

1. Lemons and limes grow on those trees.
2. His favorite sports are hunting and fishing.
3. Jeff didn't help us, nor did Walter.
4. Should we go to the movies or watch TV?
5. I wrote her letters and called her on the phone.
6. Neither Pam nor Ramona joined the team.

B. A conjunction can join parts of a subject. When it does, the subject is called a **compound subject.**

compound subject ⟶ Jesse **and** Susan took a hike.

Copy each sentence. Circle the conjunction. Underline the two words of each compound subject.

1. The dogs and cats were fighting.
2. Sam or Dave will be the lead singer.
3. Blue and green are your color choices.
4. Maples and oaks are his favorite trees.
5. His mother and father live in Florida.
6. Sofia or Samantha will be the baby's name.
7. Drums and guitars were in the store window.
8. Soft drinks and crackers were served.

C.

A conjunction can join parts of a predicate. When it does, the predicate is called a **compound predicate.**

compound predicate ⟶ They wore backpacks **and** carried walking sticks.

Copy each sentence. Circle the conjunction. Underline the two words or phrases of each compound predicate.

1. We can drive or walk to the market.
2. The cat ran outdoors and climbed a tree.
3. The autumn leaves changed color and fell.
4. Should Byron watch TV or study now?
5. That station plays music and reports the news.
6. Tina planted seeds and pulled weeds.
7. The driver can go on or stop here.
8. Will the rose bush bloom or die?

D.

One sentence can have several compound parts. It can have a compound subject, a compound predicate, or both.

compound subject ⟶ Jean **and** I are neighbors.

compound predicate ⟶ Jean drove downtown **and** went to lunch.

compound subject and predicate ⟶ Jean **and** I walked to the mall **and** went to a movie.

Copy each sentence. Circle the conjunctions. Underline the words that make up a *compound subject*, a *compound predicate*, or *both*.

1. Kate and Andy like green salads for lunch.
2. Those men and women came early and stayed late.
3. Gerald put on his helmet and rode his bike.

Lesson 43 Simple Sentences

simple sentence a group of words with one subject and one predicate that expresses a complete thought

Every sentence must have a verb. A group of words without a verb is not a sentence. A sentence must also have a subject. The subject can be a noun or a pronoun. A **simple sentence** has one subject and one predicate.

> Grandfather trimmed the bushes.
>
> I watched.
>
> Speak!

Reminder

In sentences that give a command, the subject is often understood to be *you*.

A. Sometimes a group of words includes a subject and a predicate. It might look like a sentence, but it is not. The group of words must make sense. It must be able to stand alone and express a complete thought.

> a sentence ⟶ I drove the car.
>
> not a sentence ⟶ While I drove the car.

Read each group of words. Is it a sentence? Is it only part of a sentence? If so, change the group of words into a sentence. You may add words or take away words. Write a new sentence.

1. The beautiful red flowers.
2. Cleaning the house.
3. As Sara walked to school.
4. Jody has a horse.
5. Come in!
6. If I had a million dollars.
7. Until vacation starts.
8. Bill wanted more.
9. After Donna laughed.
10. Close the door, please.

B. A simple sentence can have compound parts.

subject ⟶ **Don and Maria** studied.

predicate ⟶ Don **read and did math problems.**

subject and predicate ⟶ **Don and Maria studied and then went swimming.**

Read the subjects in the first box. Read the predicates in the second box. Choose a subject and a predicate to use in a sentence of your own. If you wish, add adjectives, articles, and adverbs. Write nine sentences (1–9).

Reminder

Adjectives and adverbs are words that describe.

Subjects	
my sister and I	elephants and rhinos
cars and bikes	Thomas
Joan and Mike	pretty birds
black cats and red cats	my father
baseball and swimming	

Predicates	
danced	are at the zoo
lie in the sun	enjoyed the dinner
got up early and played golf	sing songs
are summer sports	wrote letters
are sold and rented here	

Copy each sentence. Circle the subject. Underline the predicate. The first one is done for you.

The tree dropped its leaves.
(The tree) *dropped its leaves.*

11. He ate soup.
12. The child plays with a truck.
13. I love tomatoes.
14. Edmund climbed the mountain.
15. Thomas flew a kite in the rain.
16. London is a foggy city.
17. The hammer is in the tool box.
18. We ate pizza for dinner.
19. José rode his bike.
20. They practiced for two hours.

Lesson 44 Compound Sentences

Words to Know

compound sentence a sentence made up of two simple sentences joined by a conjunction

A **compound sentence** has two complete simple sentences joined by a conjunction. Each part of the compound sentence could stand alone.

Reminder

If you need help with simple sentences, look back at Lesson 43. If you need help with conjunctions, look back at lesson 42.

A. You know that every sentence has its own predicate and its own subject. How can you recognize a compound sentence? Look for a subject and a predicate in each simple sentence.

A Compound Sentence

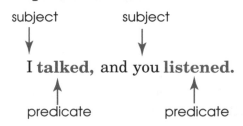

subject   subject
 ↓   ↓

I **talked,** and you **listened.**
      ↑   ↑
  predicate   predicate

***Not* a Compound Sentence**

subject   compound predicate
 ↓   ↓

Barbara **read the chapter, but did not remember it.**

Copy each compound sentence. Underline the two simple sentences.

1. Annie read a letter and wrote one back.
2. Kyle took Karly's picture, but Karly didn't smile.
3. Roger made a puppet, and he used it in a show.
4. Stan finds the leak, and Carlos fixes it.
5. The clown blew up the balloons, and the kids laughed.
6. The lion tamer cracked the whip, and the lions jumped.
7. The sails were up, but there was no wind.
8. Skip will have to get better, or we can't go.

B. Always use a comma before the conjunction in a compound sentence.

> We fished all day, **but** we caught nothing.

Rewrite each compound sentence. Put a comma where it is needed.

1. We will go shopping and you will get a coat.
2. I rode my bike and Kristine followed on skates.
3. Tina and Bill ordered salad but Jo ordered soup.
4. Doug wrote to the manager for he was upset.
5. Michelle did not see the comet nor did Rosie.
6. Rocco finished studying so he went to bed.
7. Lisette did not take notes yet she did not forget anything.
8. The show started and the crowd grew quiet.

C. You can put two simple sentences together to make a compound sentence. To do that, add a comma and a conjunction.

two simple ⟶ Mindy made the iced tea. Terry made
sentences the sandwiches.

compound ⟶ Mindy made the iced tea, **and** Terry
sentence made the sandwiches.

Read each pair of simple sentences below. Write a new sentence. Add a comma and a conjunction to make a compound sentence.

1. Eve went to the restaurant. Phil ate at home.
2. The car's brakes needed work. Kurt took the car to the brake shop.
3. Rod wanted a new apartment. He read the ads in the paper.
4. Mom drove the car. I had to walk to school.
5. His sister spilled the milk. Then she dropped her spoon.
6. Charlotte followed the recipe. The cake didn't turn out well.
7. The crowd cheered. The Penquins had won the championship.
8. We tried to sell our old bikes. No one came to buy them.

Reminder

The words *and, or, but, nor, for, so,* and *yet* are conjunctions.

Glossary

adjective a part of speech that describes a noun or pronoun: **hot** day, **yellow** rose *page 64*

adjective modifier an adverb that describes an adjective: **very** young, **extremely** busy *page 76*

adverb a part of speech that describes a verb: slowly, very, somewhat *pages 56, 74*

adverb modifier an adverb that describes or limits another adverb: **quite** rapidly *page 78*

antecedent the noun or group of nouns that a pronoun replaces: I like **sugar** because **it** tastes sweet. *pages 30, 36*

apostrophe (') a punctuation mark used to form possessive nouns and other word forms: children's *page 28*

article the most common adjectives are the articles a, an, and the *page 64*

capital letter a letter written in upper case: Jane *page 2*

colon (:) a punctuation mark used to show that a list or an example will follow: Here is what I will bring: plates, spoons, and forks. *page 18*

comma (,) a punctuation mark that tells when to pause between words or word groups: Before six in the morning, the alarm went off. January 1, 1950 *pages 8, 10*

common noun a word that names any person, place, thing, event, or idea; A common noun begins with a lowercase letter: student, school, lake, concert *page 22*

comparative adjective an adjective used to compare two or more nouns or pronouns: better, finest *page 70*

complete date a date that shows month, day, and year: December 25, 1933 *page 16*

compound predicate two or more connected verbs that have the same subject: The baby **laughed and smiled.** *page 84*

compound sentence a sentence made up of two simple sentences joined by a conjunction: The ant worked, **but** the grasshopper played. *page 88*

compound subject two or more connected subjects that have the same verb: The **balls and bats** are over there. *page 84*

conjunction a part of speech used to join words, groups of words, and sentences: and, but, or *page 84*

consonants all letters of the alphabet that are not vowels: j, l, m *page 26*

contraction a shortened form of two words in which an apostrophe (') takes the place of the missing letter or letters: don't (do not), can't (cannot) *page 82*

demonstrative pronoun a pronoun that points out nouns or other pronouns: this, that *page 38*

direct object the noun or pronoun that *receives* the action of a verb: He kissed the **baby**. *page 62*

direct quotation the exact words a person said: **"I want to go to college,"** Bill said. *page 14*

double negative the mistaken use of two negatives instead of one to tell one negative idea: **don't** need **nothing** *page 82*

exclamation point (!) a mark that shows a sentence has strong feeling: Fire! *page 6*

future tense verb a verb that tells of action or being in the future: will vote, shall go *page 58*

helping verb the part of a verb phrase that helps the main verb tell what happens or is: **is** talking, **was** sleeping, **can** bark, **might** notice *pages 50, 60*

hyphen (-) a punctuation mark used to join words together: twenty-one, one-fourth, maid-of-honor *page 18*

indefinite pronoun a pronoun that stands for a noun that is not known: anybody, someone, neither *page 36*

indirect object noun or pronoun *to whom* or *for whom* an action is done: She baked **you** a cake. *page 62*

indirect quotation what a person said, but not in the speaker's exact words: Bill said **that he wanted to go to college.** *page 14*

interrogative pronoun a pronoun used to ask a question: **who, what** *page 38*

introductory words words that begin a sentence: **In a little while,** we will know the answer. *page 12*

irregular not usual *page 26*

irregular comparative adjective an adjective that does not form the comparative by adding *-er* or *-est*: **more** interesting, **least** amusing, **worst, better** *page 72*

irregular past tense verb a word that does not form the past tense by adding *-ed* or *-d* to the present tense form: eat/ate, drive/drove *page 48*

irregular plural noun a noun that does not form the plural by just adding *-s* or *-es*: pony/ponies, half/halves, woman/women, sheep/sheep *page 26*

linking verb a word that tells what is or seems to be; a linking verb connects a noun or pronoun with another word in the sentence: Tina **is** my best friend. *pages 42, 66*

main verb the part of a verb phrase that tells about action or being: is **running**, was **sleeping** *page 50*

modify to tell more about a word; expand or limit its meaning *page 80*

negative one or more words that mean *no* or deny something: **not, no one** *page 82*

not a word that denies something or says the opposite. *Not* gives an opposite meaning to a sentence: I do understand. I do **not** understand. *page 56*

noun a part of speech that names a person, place, thing, event, or idea: John, game, victory *page 20*

noun of address a person's name used when speaking directly to that person: **Bruce,** would you like to go to the movies? *page 12*

objective pronoun a personal pronoun that *receives* an action: The ball hit **him.** *page 30*

past tense verb a word that expresses action or being that has already happened: asked, wondered, were *page 46*

pause to slow down for a moment without stopping *page 8*

period (.) a dot at the end of a sentence: Birds fly. *page 2*

personal pronoun a word that takes the place of a certain place or thing: he, we, them, it, him *page 30*

place name name of a place that has two or more words such as a city and its state or country: Atlanta, Georgia; London, England *page 16*

possessive noun a noun that shows ownership or relationship: **woman's** jacket, **Katy's** brother *page 28*

possessive pronoun a pronoun that shows ownership or relationship: my, his, theirs *page 34*

predicate the part of a sentence that tells what the subject *does* or *is:* The basketball game **was very exciting.** *page 4*

present tense verb a word that expresses action or being in the present time (now): dance, are *page 44*

proper adjective an adjective formed from a proper noun; a proper adjective describes a specific person, place, thing, event, or idea: She loves Italian food. *page 68*

proper noun a word that names a specific person, place, thing, event, or idea; a proper noun begins with a capital letter: Janet, Ohio, Super Bowl XX *page 22*

punctuation marks in a sentence to make writing clearer; includes quotation marks, commas, exclamation points, question marks, and periods: "Hey," Bill shouted. "Over here!" *page 6*

question mark (?) a mark that shows a sentence is a question: What is your name? *page 6*

quotation a sentence that shows what someone has said: **"Good afternoon,"** said the clerk. *page 14*

quotation marks (" ") the punctuation marks used to set off a direct quotation: "Let's forget it," said Myra. *page 14*

reflexive pronoun a pronoun that refers to a noun or pronoun in the same sentence: The boys helped **themselves** to the ice cream. *page 32*

regular past tense verb a word that forms the past tense by adding *-ed* or *-d*: wave/waved, dance/danced *page 46*

regular plural noun a word that ends in *-s* or *-es* and names more than one person, place, thing, event, or idea: students, rooms, cars *page 24*

semicolon (;) a punctuation mark that shows a long pause but not an end to a sentence: I was hungry; you fed me. *page 18*

sentence a group of words that makes sense: The boys built a tree house. *page 2*

series three or more words or groups of words in a row: planes, boats, and trains *page 10*

set off to separate one part of a sentence from another part: You will, **I think,** want to sign up soon. *page 12*

simple sentence a group of words with one subject and one predicate that expresses a complete thought: Birds chirp. *page 86*

singular noun a word that names just one person, place, thing, event, or idea: student, room, car *page 24*

subject the part of a sentence that tells who or what the sentence is about: **The basketball game** was very exciting. *page 4*

subjective pronoun a personal pronoun that *performs* an action: **He** caught the ball. *page 30*

tense the verb form that shows the *time* of the verb's action or being—past, present, or future: drive, drove, will drive *page 44*

***to be* verb phrase** a verb phrase that uses *am, is, are, was,* or *were* as a helping verb: am running, were hoping *page 50*

***to do* verb** a verb that is formed from the verb *to do:* do, did, does *page 54*

***to do* verb phrase** a verb phrase that uses *do, did,* or *does* as a helping verb: did grow, does understand *page 54*

***to have* verb** a verb that is formed from the verb *to have:* have, has, had *page 52*

***to have* verb phrase** a verb phrase that uses *have, has,* or *had* as a helping verb: has talked, has come *page 52*

verb the part of speech that expresses action or being: run, are *page 40*

verb phrase a main verb and a helping verb that act as one verb: am thinking, was growing *page 50*

vowels the letters a, e, i, o, u, and sometimes y *page 46*